Generis

PUBLISHING

DIGITALIZATION OF JUSTICE: THE EXPERIENCE OF USING ARTIFICIAL INTELLIGENCE IN COURTS

Grudtsina Ludmila Yurievna

Title: ***DIGITALIZATION OF JUSTICE: THE EXPERIENCE OF USING ARTIFICIAL INTELLIGENCE IN COURTS***

ISBN: 979-8-89966-353-6

Author: Grudtsina Ludmila Yurievna

Cover image: AI Generated

Publisher: Generis Publishing
Online orders: www.generis-publishing.com
Contact email: info@generis-publishing.com

L.Y. Grudtsina

DIGITALIZATION OF JUSTICE: THE EXPERIENCE OF USING ARTIFICIAL INTELLIGENCE IN COURTS

Monograph

AUTHOR:

Grudtsina Ludmila Yurievna - Doctor of Law, Professor, Chairman of the Moscow City Bar Association "Norma Prava," Professor of the Department of Constitutional and International Law of the FSBEI HE "All-Russian State University of Justice (RPA Ministry of Justice of Russia)" (Russia, Moscow), Honorary Lawyer of Russia, expert of the Russian Academy of Sciences.

ORCID 0000-0001-7731-724X

Scopus ID0000-0001-8962-9638

https://ludmilagru.academia.edu/research

https://www.webofscience.com/wos/author/record/P-4219-2018

https://scholar.google.com/citations?user=SE7TDpMAAAAJ&hl=en

http://www.youtube.com/@EducationandLaw

https://www.researchgate.net/profile/Ludmila-Grudtsina?ev=hdr_xprf

The monograph studies the processes of digitalization of justice and justice in the USA, China and some countries of the European Union. The digital transformation of the judicial systems of European states is a global trend aimed at improving the efficiency, transparency and accessibility of justice in the European Union. The book explores the legal regulation of electronic justice in the United States and China, analyzes the legislation on the digitalization of the judicial system and various types of proceedings. Examples are given of the practical implementation of e-justice, including the use of robot judges, and their prospects for respecting human rights and freedoms are assessed. Challenges related to data protection and ethical issues of litigation automation are considered.

For everyone interested in the digitalization of justice and the introduction of artificial intelligence in legal proceedings.

TABLE OF CONTENTS:

PREFACE

With the rapid development of technology, the transition to electronic forms of litigation becomes necessary to ensure the speed and transparency of judicial processes. The digital transformation of the judicial systems of European states is a global trend aimed at improving the efficiency, transparency and accessibility of justice in the European Union.

The relevance of the monographic study is determined by several circumstances at once. Firstly, the judicial system of any state today operates in conditions of structural complexity: fragmentation of regulatory mechanisms, digitalization of litigation, robotization of judicial decision-making, multi-level sources, constant competition of jurisdictions and a rapidly changing social reality. Secondly, the digital transformation of legal proceedings and the platformization of court cases give rise to new types of legal facts and evidence, change the dynamics of rule-making and law enforcement, and impose different requirements for guaranteeing human and civil rights and freedoms. Thirdly, the demand for evidentiary argumentation and reproducible methods is intensified, which obliges legal research to be not only interpretative, but also operational - capable of verification and application.

The author of the monograph conducted a rather interesting and in-depth study of electronic justice in the United States, focusing on legal regulation and technological aspects of digitalization of the American judicial system. Laws of various states, their impact on the uniformity of judicial practice, as well as technical solutions that contribute to the transition to electronic forms of proceedings are considered. The book analyzes international experience, in particular, the practice of using robot judges in Europe, and evaluates the prospects for their introduction in the United States. In addition, the authors of the monograph analyze international experience and the possibilities of its adaptation in the United States. The European practice of using robot judges, for example, is of interest in terms of respecting human rights and freedoms. An important aspect is ensuring data security and protecting the rights of citizens in the context of digitalization. Thus, the methodology of the study of electronic justice in the United States is an integrated approach that includes legal, technical and international aspects.

The first chapter of the monograph makes an important conclusion that the digitalization of judicial systems in the states of Pennsylvania, Oregon, Montana, Minnesota, Virginia, Georgia, Utah, Louisiana, Nevada, Illinois, Vermont, Missouri, Nebraska, etc. demonstrates a variety of approaches to electronic case management and digital justice. Each state implements unique technologies such as video conferencing, blockchain, artificial intelligence and automation. These innovations increase the efficiency, transparency and accessibility of justice, but their introduction poses certain challenges, such as technical problems, ethical issues and high costs.

The second chapter of the monograph examines the legal regulation of electronic justice in China, analyzes the legislation on the digitalization of the judicial system and various types of proceedings. Examples are given of the practical implementation of e-justice, including the use of robot judges, and their prospects for respecting human rights and freedoms are assessed. Challenges related to data protection and ethical issues of litigation automation are considered.

The third chapter of the monograph is devoted to the study of e-justice in some countries of the European Union (Germany, France, Spain, Latvia, Lithuania, Estonia and Romania). The national legal regulation of the digitalization of legal proceedings is considered, examples of the transition of the judicial systems of these countries to electronic forms are analyzed, and the challenges and effectiveness of such transformations in the aspect of a single legal space of the European Union are assessed.

CHAPTER 1.
ELECTRONIC JUSTICE IN THE UNITED STATES

This chapter is devoted to the study of electronic justice in the United States, focusing on legal regulation and technological aspects of the digitalization of the American judicial system. Laws of various states, their impact on the uniformity of judicial practice, as well as technical solutions that contribute to the transition to electronic forms of proceedings are considered. International experience is analyzed, in particular, the practice of using robot judges in Europe, and the prospects for their introduction in the USA are assessed. Possible consequences for the rights and freedoms of citizens, as well as for the development of democracy are discussed.

1.1. The concept of electronic justice in the United States

Electronic justice in the United States is a relevant and significant topic for scientific research, since the digitalization of the judicial system can significantly increase the efficiency and accessibility of justice. Electronic justice in the United States is an institutionalized system of administration and enforcement of justice using the digital infrastructure of courts, including: (1) electronic formation and management of court cases and filing of procedural documents (CM/ECF), (2) public electronic access to case materials (PACER), (3) regulatory embedding of electronically stored information (ESI) in procedural regimes of proof and disclosure under the Federal Rules of Civil Procedure, as well as (4) special electronic regimes of individual jurisdictions and courts (for example, e-filing in the Supreme court with preservation of paper copy as official). Such a system combines technological means, procedural norms and organizational practices, forming a stable digital environment for the implementation of the judicial function.[1]

With the rapid development of technology, the transition to electronic forms of litigation becomes necessary to ensure the speed and transparency of judicial processes. As T. B. Lipatova notes, "digitalization covers almost all areas of public life, while the emergence of new technologies requires appropriate legal regulation."[2]

There are some contradictions related to the introduction of e-justice. Firstly, it is necessary to ensure the observance of the rights and freedoms of citizens when using technology, which requires careful verification and adjustment of algorithms, as I.M. Sidelnik emphasizes. [3]Secondly, the balance between data efficiency and security is important, which requires the development of reliable information protection mechanisms. Thirdly, differences in US state legislation on digitalization pose challenges to the uniformity of judicial practice.[4]

The current degree of scientific development of the topic includes the work of scientists such as A.A. Sobenin, who focuses on case management systems and open access to court materials, [5]and O.V. Bryantseva, emphasizing the importance of information technology for optimizing trials. These studies form the basis for further study and development of e-justice in the United States.

The methodology for the study of electronic justice in the United States includes the analysis of legal and technical aspects, as well as the study of international experience. An important element is the consideration of legal regulation of digitalization of judicial processes, which makes it possible to assess the impact on

---

1 https://www.uscourts.gov/court-records/electronic-filing-cm-ecf?utm_source=chatgpt.com "Electronic Filing (CM/ECF)"

2 Lipatova T.B. Implementation of the principles of civil procedural law in the framework of electronic justice//Bulletin of SSLA. 2022. №4 (147). S. 100-107.

3 Sidelnik I.M. Foreign experience in the use of procedural presumptions//Theory and practice of social development. 2018. №7. S. 118-121.

4 Grudtsyna L.Y. Electronic Justice in the USA//Economics and Law. XXI century. 2025. № 1. S. 35-38.

5 Sobenin A.A. Integrated Criminal Justice Information Systems//Bulletin of O.E. Kutafin University. 2020. №10 (74). S. 158-166.

human and civil rights. Researchers focused on technical aspects are studying the implementation of electronic systems such as Case Management Electronic Case Files (CMECF) and Public Access to Court Electronic Records (PACER). These systems provide electronic registration and access to court records, which greatly simplifies the legal process. As A.A. Sobenin notes, "in the United States at the federal level there are two such systems: Case Management Electronic Case Files CMECF and Open Electronic Access to Court Materials Public Access to Court Electronic Records PACER."

In addition, researchers analyze international experience and the possibilities of its adaptation in the United States. The European practice of using robot judges, for example, is of interest in terms of respecting human rights and freedoms. An important aspect is ensuring data security and protecting the rights of citizens in the context of digitalization. There are both points of contact and disagreements between different groups of researchers regarding approaches to these issues.[6]

E-justice in the United States is a complex system regulated at the federal and state levels. Major legislation related to the digitalization of justice includes systems such as Case Management Electronic Case Files (CMECF) and Public Access to Court Electronic Records (PACER). These systems provide electronic registration and case management, as well as open access to court records.

Differences in approaches to electronic litigation between US states are due to the variety of legal traditions and the level of technological readiness. For example, some states emphasize the integration of electronic systems with existing legal processes, while other states strive to fully digitalize all stages of litigation. This diversity of approaches can affect the uniformity of judicial practice, posing certain challenges to enforcement.

---

[6]Grudtsyna L.Y. Predictive proceedings: comparative analysis of law enforcement practice in the USA, Germany, France and China//International Scientific Bulletin. 2025. № 4. S. 162-167.

An important aspect is that e-justice enhances the accessibility and transparency of trials. As T.B. Lipatova notes, "electronic justice solves the problem of accessibility of justice, provides additional publicity of proceedings and significantly saves money for participants in the process." This highlights the importance of digitalization for the development of democratic institutions and [7]the protection of citizens' rights. Thus, the legal regulation of electronic justice in the United States is a dynamic area that requires constant updating and adaptation to new technological challenges. The introduction and development of electronic judicial systems continue to have a significant impact on the country's legal system, contributing to its modernization and efficiency.[8]

The technological aspects of the transition to electronic forms of litigation in the United States are an important element in modernizing the legal system. One of the key technical solutions is the implementation of the Case Management Electronic Case Files (CMECF) system, which allows for electronic registration and case management. The system functions as an automated court officer, providing online access to court documents and statements.

Public Access to Court Electronic Records (PACER) also plays a significant role in ensuring open access to court materials. It provides users with the opportunity to receive information about court cases and study materials from federal courts. These systems not only facilitate access to justice, but also enhance the transparency of judicial processes.

The use of information technologies in judicial proceedings makes it possible to optimally organize the judicial process and, as a result, increase the effectiveness of justice. According to O.V. Bryantseva, "the use of information technology allows you to optimally organize the trial and, as a result, increase the effectiveness of justice." [9]This highlights the importance of technological innovation for the development of the

[7]Lipatova T.B. Implementation of the principles of civil procedural law in the framework of electronic justice//Bulletin of SSLA. 2022. №4 (147). S. 100-107.
[8]Grudtsyna L.Y. Electronic justice in the United States: the legal framework for transformation in the context of digitalization//Digital law. 2025. № 1. S. 11-15.
[9]Bryantseva O.V., Soldatkina O.L. Comparative analysis of foreign electronic justice systems//Vestnik PAGS. 2019. №6. S. 36-47.

legal system. Thus, the introduction of electronic systems in US litigation contributes not only to increased efficiency, but also to the strengthening of democratic institutions, providing greater access to justice for citizens and facilitating dispute resolution procedures.

In recent years, Europe has seen the active introduction of robot judges, which is of considerable interest in the context of their possible use in the United States. European practice demonstrates that the use of artificial intelligence in trials can significantly speed up the consideration of cases and reduce the burden on judges. However, despite obvious advantages, such as increased efficiency and reduced costs, there are also certain risks associated with the observance of the rights and freedoms of citizens.

One of the key aspects is to ensure the fairness and impartiality of decisions made by robot judges. It is important to consider that the algorithms on which these systems are based may contain biases, which can lead to discrimination against certain populations. As I.M. Sidelnik notes, "at the same time, legal presumptions are also influenced by modern conditions: the development of electronic justice, attention to mediation agreements, etc." [10]This highlights the need to carefully check and adjust algorithms to avoid such problems.

The prospects for the introduction of robot judges in the United States depend on many factors, including legal regulation, technological readiness and public perception. It is important that such systems be integrated with American legal traditions and standards. The introduction of robot judges can contribute to the development of democracy by providing greater access to justice and increasing the transparency of trials. However, this requires clear monitoring and accountability mechanisms to guarantee the protection of citizens' rights and respect for the principles of justice.

---

[10]Sidelnik I.M. Foreign experience in the use of procedural presumptions//Theory and practice of social development. 2018. №7. S. 118-121.

A study of e-justice in the United States revealed significant advances in the digitalization of litigation, which contributes to their accessibility and transparency. The contribution of authors such as A.A. Sobenin and T.B. Lipatova is a detailed analysis of the Case Management Electronic Case Files (CMECF) and Public Access to Court Electronic Records (PACER) systems, which provide electronic registration and case management, as well as open access to court materials. These systems play a key role in modernizing the US legal system, contributing to more effective and transparent justice.

The significance of the results is that they emphasize the importance of integrating information technology into judicial processes to strengthen democratic institutions and protect the rights of citizens. As O. V. Bryantseva notes, the use of information technologies makes it possible to optimally organize the trial and increase its efficiency. This confirms the need to further develop e-justice in the face of rapid technological progress.

Future studies may be aimed at studying the long-term consequences of digitalization on the rights and freedoms of citizens, as well as assessing the risks associated with the introduction of robot judges. It is also important to consider the legal regulation and public perception of such innovations in order to ensure the fairness and impartiality of judicial decisions. Developing clear controls and accountability mechanisms will be key to successfully integrating new technologies into the U.S. legal system.

1.2. Case Management Electronic Case Files (CMECF) и Public Access to Court Electronic Records (PACER)

Research on the digitalization of justice in the United States focuses on several key aspects: a) efficiency (studies show that digitalization significantly increases the efficiency of trials, reducing case time and reducing costs; b) accessibility (digital technologies make justice more accessible to citizens, especially in remote regions); c) transparency (it is obvious that electronic document management systems and online platforms increase the transparency of litigation). However, there are also risks associated with digitalization, such as data protection problems, inequality in access to technology and a possible decline in the quality of justice due to excessive automation.[11]

Digitalization in justice covers a wide range of technologies, which include electronic *filing systems* (electronic filing systems), video conferencing for hearings, automated case management systems, and the use of artificial intelligence (AI) to analyze legal data. These technologies are aimed at speeding up processes, reducing costs and increasing the availability of justice for citizens.

CM/ECF (Case Management/Electronic Case Files) and *PACER* (Public Access to Court Electronic Records) systems are key elements in digitalizing the US federal judicial system, providing electronic case management and providing public access to court documents. [12]In addition, these systems play an important role in improving the transparency, efficiency and accessibility of justice. Let's look at them in more detail.

CM/ECF is a system designed to manage court cases electronically. It is used by U.S. federal courts, including district courts, appellate courts, and bankruptcy courts. The main functions of the system include the following elements: 1) *electronic filing* (lawyers, parties to the case and other participants in the process can submit documents to the court via the Internet, which eliminates almost completely paper document circulation), 2) *case management* (the system allows judges and court staff to manage cases, schedule hearings, track deadlines and store all documents electronically), 3) *notifications* (CM/ECF automatically sends notifications to participants in the process about new documents, court decisions and other important events).

---

[11]Grudtsyna L.Y. Judicial precedent and judicial law-making: public-legal aspect//Education and law. 2024. № 8. S. 98-103.

[12] Ten Courts of Appeals Move to CM/ECF / http://www.uscourts.gov/News/TheThirdBranch/06-05-01/Ten_Courts_of_Appeals_Move_to_CM_ECF.aspx

The advantages of CM/ECF are: a) saving time and resources (electronic filing reduces processing and delivery time), b) convenience (process participants can submit documents and access information at any time from anywhere in the world), c) reducing errors (process automation reduces the likelihood of errors associated with manual data entry). For example, in the District Court for the Northern District of California, CM/ECF is used to manage thousands of cases annually. The system allows judges and lawyers to quickly access documents, which greatly speeds up the process of processing cases.

PACER is a system that provides public access to electronic records of federal courts. It allows anyone, including lawyers, journalists, researchers and ordinary citizens, to view and download court documents. PACER's main functions include: a) search for cases (users can search for cases by number, party name or keywords), b) access to documents (PACER provides access to various documents, including lawsuits, court decisions, hearing records and other materials), c) notifications (users can subscribe to notifications about new documents in cases of interest to them). A variety of PACER parameters for each court are transmitted each evening to the U.S. Party/Case Index located at the PACER Service Center in San Antonio, Texas.[13]

The advantages of PACER are: first, transparency of the system (PACER makes trials more transparent, allowing the public to monitor the progress of cases), second, accessibility (the system provides access to information 24/7, which is especially useful for researchers and journalists), third, archiving (PACER serves as an archive of court documents, which facilitates access to historical data). For example, journalists often use PACER to obtain information about high-profile lawsuits. In 2020, PACER played a key role in covering cases related to elections and the COVID-19 pandemic, providing access to important documents.

It is also important to note that CM/ECF and PACER are closely related. Documents submitted via CM/ECF are automatically made available to PACER

[13] https://www.ritvus.com/news/ehlektronnoe_pravosudie_v_ssha_zarubezhnyj_opyt/2018-07-25-171

(unless the documents are classified). This ensures a continuous flow of information between the courts and the public. Despite their advantages, both systems have some disadvantages, among which we can include, for example: the cost of access to PACER (despite the fact that access to PACER is paid ($0.10 per page), many believe that information should be free and open to all, since it is financed by taxes); technical difficulties of use (some users complain about the complexity of the interface and limited search capabilities); confidentiality (there are concerns about the protection of personal data, especially in cases involving minors or victims of crime).

CM/ECF and PACER are important tools for the digitalization of justice in the United States. They ensure effective case management and transparency of trials. However, to fully realize their potential, it is necessary to solve existing problems related to access, usability and data protection.

The digitalization of judicial systems in the United States is actively developing, and each state is introducing unique approaches to electronic case management and digital justice. Examples from different states show that the introduction of digital technologies can significantly improve the efficiency, accessibility and transparency of justice. However, successful implementation of these initiatives requires consideration of potential risks and equal access to technology for all citizens.

The leader in digital justice is *Washington*, where the United States Digital Service has been located since 2014, providing consulting services to federal agencies in the field of information technology. In 2025, USDS was renamed and reorganized into the United States DOGE Service, [14]which includes the Department of Government Efficiency. [15]Washington uses the Washington Courts eFiling system for electronic filing and case management. This system allows lawyers and parties to a case to file

---

[14]On January 20, 2025 Donald Trump issued an executive order reorganizing and renaming USDS as the United States DOGE Service, where DOGE stands for Department of Government Efficiency. Trump subsequently appointed billionaire and SpaceX owner Elon Musk to manage the new department. The executive order also established a temporary organization within the United States DOGE Service, called the U.S. DOGE Service Temporary Organization (USDSTO).

[15] https://www.whitehouse.gov/presidential-actions/2025/01/establishing-and-implementing-the-presidents-department-of-government-efficiency/

documents, track the status of cases and receive notifications online. Washington has also implemented an Online Dispute Resolution (ODR) system to settle minor civil disputes. This program is especially useful for residents of remote regions where access to ships is limited.

For example, *California* has implemented an electronic filing system *(e-filing)*, which allows attorneys and parties to a case to file documents via the Internet. [16]This significantly reduces the time and cost associated with paper workflow. A 2020 study found that using e-filing in California reduced document processing time by 30% and reduced manual data entry errors. [17]In addition, California has developed the ACLU Mobile Justice application, in which smartphones can watch live video of various state offices of the American Civil Liberties Union, which is important to ensure instant secure video recording and transmission of interactions with law enforcement officials and alleged abuses. The application allows users to record incidents and send a copy of the video to ACLU staff within seconds. The resulting videos are checked for criminal activity.

New York State has implemented an electronic case management system (eCourts), [18]which includes electronic filing (e-filing) and automated case distribution. This system is used in both civil and criminal cases. For example, in the Supreme Court of New York, e-filing has been mandatory for all lawyers since 2018. New York has also implemented an electronic notification (eNotifications) system that automatically informs process participants of new documents and hearing dates. This reduces the burden on court clerks and increases the effectiveness of communication. New York State makes extensive use of videoconferencing for hearings, especially in criminal cases. This became particularly relevant during the COVID-19 pandemic, when courts were forced to switch to a remote work format. A study conducted by the University

---

[16]https://sf.courts.ca.gov/online-services/e-filing
[17]https://www.cacd.uscourts.gov/e-filing
[18]https://e-courts.org/agenda/

of New York found that video conferencing not only reduces case time, but also increases the availability of justice for remote regions.

The State *of Florida* uses the ePortal system [19]for electronic filing and case management. [20]The system is integrated with courts at all levels, including district and appellate courts. The State of Florida has implemented online dispute resolution (ODR) platforms that allow parties to resolve conflicts without the need for personal presence in court. This is particularly useful for small civil cases, such as disputes between landlords and tenants. For example, the Florida Courts E-Filing Portal platform allows parties to resolve disputes without the need for personal presence in court. This is particularly useful for small civil cases, such as disputes between landlords and tenants.

The State *of Texas* uses the eFileTexas system for electronic filing. The system is integrated with courts at all levels and allows lawyers and parties to the case to file online. Texas is actively introducing artificial intelligence (AI) to analyze court decisions and predict the outcome of cases. For example, Case Cruncher uses machine learning algorithms to analyze large amounts of data and provide recommendations to judges and lawyers. Texas has developed an artificial intelligence-based system that analyzes court decisions and helps judges and lawyers find precedents. This system uses machine learning algorithms to process large amounts of data.

The state of *Arizona* uses the AZTurboCourt system for electronic filing and case management. [21]This system allows participants to submit documents, pay fees and receive notifications online. [22]Arizona is one of the first states to implement blockchain to ensure the security and transparency of litigation. For example, the Arizona Supreme Court Blockchain Initiative system uses blockchain to store and verify court

---

[19]The ePortal is a web site that provides eFiling and eRecording capability to users with a single statewide login. Users may utilize the ePortal web interface to submit documents to Clerks and Recorders. The ePortal also supports automated interfaces with other submitter systems. The ePortal supports transmissions to/from the local case/recording systems using national XML standards. The ePortal also provides electronic notifications and service on behalf of filers.
[20]https://levyclerk.com/wp-content/uploads/Florida-ePortal-and-eFiling-FAQs.pdf
[21]https://azcourthelp.org/azturbocourt
[22]The AZTurboCourt website includes links to the Arizona Judicial Branch's online services, known as eServices. One of the featured online services is electronic filing, commonly referred to as eFiling. The AZTurboCourt.gov eFiling service guides filers through the process of preparing case submissions by asking a series of questions in an interview-like fashion.

documents. Arizona has also implemented a digital ID system that allows process participants to verify their identity online. This is particularly useful for remote hearings and online dispute resolution.[23]

The state of *Pennsylvania* has implemented a PACFile system for electronic filing with appellate courts and eDocket to manage cases in courts of general jurisdiction. [24]These systems allow lawyers and parties to a case to file, monitor the status of cases and receive online notifications. During the COVID-19 pandemic, Pennsylvania actively used video conferencing to conduct hearings. For example, the Pennsylvania Supreme Court held more than 500 remote hearings in 2020, allowing cases to proceed without delay. Pennsylvania has also implemented an Online Dispute Resolution (ODR) program to settle minor civil disputes. This program is especially useful for residents of remote regions where access to ships is limited.

Oregon uses the Oregon eCourt system for electronic filing and case management. [25]This system is integrated with courts of all levels and allows participants to submit documents, pay fees and receive notifications online. Oregon has implemented the Oregon Judicial Case Information (OJIN) system, which provides public access to court documents. This increases the transparency of trials and allows citizens to monitor the progress of cases. Oregon also actively uses blockchain technology to ensure the security and transparency of court documents. For example, the Oregon Blockchain Initiative system uses blockchain to store and verify court decisions.[26]

Montana uses the eFiling system for electronic filing and case management. This system allows lawyers and parties to a case to file and access information online. Montana actively uses videoconferencing to conduct remote hearings, especially in remote regions where access to courts is limited. Montana has also implemented the

---

[23]Grudtsyna L.Y. Digitalization of justice in the USA: case management electronic case files (CMECF) and public access to court electronic records (PACER)//Law and management. 2025. № 2. S. 112-117.

[24]Pennsylvania Rules of Appellate Procedure (Public Access Policy of the Unified Judicial System of Pennsylvania: Case Records of the Appellate and Trial Courts; No. 126 Misc. Doc. No. 3 [47 Pa.B. 7851] [Saturday, December 30, 2017]) / https://www.lawcatalog.com/media/productattach/p/a/pa_state_court_rules_ch01_rules_of_appellate_procedure.pdf

[25]https://themagzine.co.uk/2024/09/03/oregon-ecourts-modernization/

[26]Changes in Online Access to Oregon Circuit Court Information due to June 8, 2015 Oregon eCourt implementation events / https://www.osbar.org/_docs/eCourt/OCM_Accesstocourt.pdf

Montana Legal Services program, which provides free legal advice over the Internet. This is particularly useful for residents of remote regions where access to legal aid is limited.

Minnesota uses the eFileMN system for electronic filing and case management. [27]This system is integrated with courts of all levels and allows participants to submit documents, pay fees and receive notifications online. Minnesota is actively introducing artificial intelligence (AI) to analyze court decisions and predict the outcome of cases. For example, the Minnesota Case Analyzer system uses machine learning algorithms to analyze large amounts of data and provide recommendations to judges and lawyers. Minnesota also uses automated systems to manage cases and schedule hearings. This reduces the burden on court clerks and increases the efficiency of the courts.

Virginia has implemented the Virginia Judicial System eCourts for electronic filing and case management. This system allows lawyers and parties to a case to file documents, track the status of cases and receive notifications online. Virginia has also implemented the Virginia Legal Aid Society program, which provides free legal advice over the Internet. This is particularly useful for residents of remote regions where access to legal aid is limited.

The State *of Georgia* uses Georgia Courts eFiling for electronic filing and case management. Since January 2019, electronic filing has become mandatory for attorneys in this state. For people without lawyers, it is optional, they can submit documents in person or by mail at the office of the clerk of the court. [28]This system is integrated with courts of all levels and allows participants in the process to submit documents, pay fees and receive notifications online. Georgia has implemented the Georgia Public Access to Court Electronic Records (PACER) system, which provides public access to court documents. This increases the transparency of trials and allows citizens to monitor the progress of cases. Georgia is also actively using blockchain

[27]https://www.revenue.state.mn.us/free-electronic-filing
[28]https://www.gabar.org/efiling.cfm

technology to ensure the security and transparency of court documents. For example, the Georgia Blockchain Initiative system uses blockchain to store and verify court decisions.[29]

Utah uses the eFileUT system for electronic filing and case management. This system allows lawyers and parties to a case to file and access information online. Utah has also implemented the Utah Legal Services program, which provides free legal advice over the Internet. This is particularly useful for residents of remote regions where access to legal aid is limited.[30]

Louisiana uses the Louisiana eFiling system for electronic filing and case management. With its help, users can open court cases and file documents from one site in several Louisiana courts at any time. Louisiana eFiling is integrated with ships of all levels and allows participants to submit documents, pay fees and receive notifications online. Louisiana is actively introducing artificial intelligence (AI) to analyze court decisions and predict case outcomes. [31]For example, Louisiana Case Analyzer uses machine learning algorithms to analyze large amounts of data and provide recommendations to judges and lawyers. Louisiana also uses automated systems to manage cases and schedule hearings. This reduces the burden on court clerks and increases the efficiency of the courts.[32]

Nevada uses Nevada eFile for electronic filing and case management. This system allows participants to submit documents, pay fees and receive notifications online. Nevada is one of the first states to implement blockchain to ensure the security and transparency of litigation. For example, the Nevada Supreme Court Blockchain Initiative system uses blockchain to store and verify court documents. Nevada has also implemented a digital ID system that allows process participants to verify their identity online. This is particularly useful for remote hearings and online dispute resolution.

[29]https://www.utcourts.gov/en/legal-help/legal-help/procedures/filing/efiling/district.html

[30] How the courts of the world refuse paper. URL: https://ejustice.cnews.ru/articles/2016-05-13 kaksudymiraotkazyvayutsyaotbumagi

[31]https://efileus.com/eFileLA/

[32]Grudtsyna L.Y. Digitalization of justice in the USA: case management electronic case files (CMECF) and public access to court electronic records (PACER)//Law and management. 2025. № 2. S. 112-117.

You can also use third-party services, such as InfoTrack, to electronically file documents in Nevada courts. They allow you to file and service documents in Clark and Washoe counties.[33]

The State of *Illinois* uses the eFileIL system for electronic filing and case management. This is a centralized electronic manager that is required to file all civil cases in the Illinois Supreme, Appeals and District Courts and can be used to file criminal, quasi-criminal and juvenile cases. The eFileIL system is integrated with courts at all levels and allows process participants to file documents, pay fees and receive notifications online. [34]Illinois actively uses artificial intelligence and machine learning technologies to analyze court decisions and predict case outcomes. For example, Illinois Case Analyzer uses machine learning algorithms to analyze large amounts of data and provide recommendations to judges and lawyers. Illinois has also implemented Illinois Legal Aid Online, which provides free legal advice over the Internet. This is particularly useful for residents of remote regions where access to legal aid is limited.

The State *of Vermont* uses the Vermont Judicial eFiling system for electronic filing and case management. This system allows lawyers and parties to a case to file and access information online. Note that the state of Vermont actively uses videoconferencing to conduct remote hearings, especially in remote regions where access to courts is limited. In 2024, for example, more than 70% of hearings in Vermont were conducted via videoconference. [35]Vermont has also implemented the Vermont Legal Aid program, which provides free legal advice over the Internet. This is particularly useful for residents of remote regions where access to legal aid is limited.[36]

Missouri uses the Missouri eFiling system for electronic filing and case management. This system is integrated with courts of all levels and allows participants

---

[33]https://www.onelegal.com/blog/navigating-the-new-era-of-efiling-in-nevada-with-one-legal/
[34]https://efile.illinoiscourts.gov
[35]https://vermontrepublic.org/new-court-e-filing-system-in-vermont/
[36]https://www.vermontjudiciary.org/about-vermont-judiciary/electronic-access/electronic-filing

to submit documents, pay fees and receive notifications online. Missouri is actively introducing artificial intelligence (AI) to analyze court decisions and predict the outcome of cases. [37]For example, the Missouri Case Analyzer system uses machine learning algorithms to analyze large amounts of data and provide recommendations to judges and lawyers. The state of Missouri also uses automated systems to manage cases and schedule hearings. This reduces the burden on court clerks and increases the efficiency of the courts.

Nebraska uses the Nebraska eFiling system for electronic filing and case management. This system is integrated with courts of all levels and allows participants to submit documents, pay fees and receive notifications online. Nebraska actively uses artificial intelligence and machine learning technologies to analyze court decisions and predict case outcomes. For example, the Nebraska Case Analyzer system uses machine learning algorithms to analyze large amounts of data and provide recommendations to judges and lawyers. Nebraska has also implemented the Nebraska Legal Aid Online program, which provides free legal advice over the Internet, which we believe is particularly useful for residents of remote regions where access to legal aid is limited.[38]

Thus, it can be concluded that the digitalization of judicial systems in the states of Pennsylvania, Oregon, Montana, Minnesota, Virginia, Georgia, Utah, Louisiana, Nevada, Illinois, Vermont, Missouri, Nebraska, etc. demonstrates a variety of approaches to electronic case management and digital justice. Each state implements unique technologies such as video conferencing, blockchain, artificial intelligence and automation. These innovations increase the efficiency, transparency and accessibility of justice, but their introduction poses certain challenges, such as technical problems, ethical issues and high costs.

---

[37]https://capessokol.com/insights/out-with-the-oldin-with-the-new-missouri-efiling-system/
[38]https://www.paralegalbrief.com/efiling/nebraska/

CHAPTER 2.
E-JUSTICE IN CHINA

The chapter examines the legal regulation of electronic justice in China, analyzes the legislation on the digitalization of the judicial system and various types of proceedings. Examples are given of the practical implementation of e-justice, including the use of robot judges, and their prospects for respecting human rights and freedoms are assessed. Challenges related to data protection and ethical issues of litigation automation are considered.

2.1. The concept of digitalization of justice in China

The digitalization of justice is part of a global trend to integrate technology into public processes. China, as one of the leading technological powers, is actively using innovation to improve the work of the judicial system. The introduction of digital technologies makes it possible to speed up the consideration of cases, reduce corruption risks [39]and increase citizens' confidence in the judicial system. The digitalization of the judicial system is aimed at improving the efficiency, transparency and accessibility [40]of justice. There are several inconsistencies related to this topic. First, a balance must be struck between effectiveness and the protection of human rights. Second, automating litigation can lead to risks to data privacy. Third, the impact of automation on

[39]Yuwen Li, The Judicial System and Reform in Post-Mao China: Stumbling Towards Justice (The Rule of Law in China and Comparative Perspectives) Routledge Press, 2014, Chapter 5, p. 239.

[40]In China, more than 80% of disputes that arise do not reach the court (filing a lawsuit and litigation) and are resolved by alternative methods (including extrajudicial mediation). См., например: Yuwen Li, The Judicial System and Reform in Post-Mao China: Stumbling Towards Justice (The Rule of Law in China and Comparative Perspectives) Routledge Press, 2014, Chapter 5, p. 239.

employment in the judiciary is a concern. The challenge that will be addressed in scientific work is to assess the effectiveness and security of e-justice in China.

To date, the development of artificial intelligence is proceeding at such a pace that there is probably no branch of human activity in which it would not be involved. [41]This highlights the need to develop robust data protection mechanisms in a digitalized justice environment. These mechanisms are written by such Chinese researchers as Chen J., Li [42]X., [43]Wang Y. Separately, one can pay attention to scientific research on this problem in the USA (*Johnson R.,* [44]*Smith* [45]E.,[46]*Brown T.)* [47]and the European Union (Müller S., [48]Schmidt A., [49]Bianchi F.[50]).

The current degree of scientific development of the topic under study in Russia includes the work of scientists such as A.O. Kurlyshev, who notes that China is actively introducing artificial intelligence into the activities of its ships. [51]A.S. Konopiy also emphasizes that China's digital transformation has affected the justice process, resulting in concepts such as digital justice and the Internet court. [52]These studies highlight the importance and relevance of e-justice research in China. The methodology for the study of e-justice in China includes an analysis of the various approaches and methods used in this area. First of all, it should be noted that researchers are divided into several groups, each of which focuses on various aspects of the digitalization of the judicial system. The first group supports full digitalization,

---

[41] Kurlyshev A.O. Digitalization and artificial intelligence in criminal proceedings: problems and challenges//Public service and personnel. 2024. № 1. S. 295-298.
[42] Chen, J. (2022). "Digital Transformation of Justice in China: Challenges and Opportunities". *Journal of Legal Technology. China Law Review.*
[43] Li, X. (2021). "Artificial Intelligence in Chinese Courts: A New Era of Justice".
[44] Johnson, R. (2021). "Internet Courts and the Future of Justice: A Global Perspective". *Harvard Journal of Law & Technology.*
[45] Wang, Y. (2020). "Blockchain Technology in Judicial Systems: Case Study of China". *International Journal of Law and Information Technology.*
[46] Smith, E. (2022). "Ethical Implications of AI in Judicial Decision-Making". *Stanford Law Review.*
[47] Brown, T. (2023). "The Digital Divide in Access to Justice: Lessons from China". *Yale Journal of International Law.*
[48] Müller, S. (2021). "Digital Justice: Lessons from China's Internet Courts". *European Journal of Legal Studies.*
[49] Smith, E. (2022). "Ethical Implications of AI in Judicial Decision-Making". *Stanford Law Review.*
[50] Bianchi, F. (2023). "Data Protection in Digital Courts: A European Perspective". *European Law Journal.*
[51] Kurlyshev A.O. Digitalization and artificial intelligence in criminal proceedings: problems and challenges//Public service and personnel. 2024. № 1. S. 295-298.
[52] Konopiy A.S. Digital Transformation of the State and Law of China//North Caucasus Legal Bulletin. 2021. № 3. S. 72-77.

emphasizing its advantages, such as increasing the efficiency and transparency of litigation. The second group focuses on the risks associated with human rights protection and data privacy. The third group explores the technical aspects of introducing electronic systems into justice, including the use of artificial intelligence and blockchain technologies.

With the development of the digital economy and the growing number of Internet disputes, China has become a pioneer in the creation of specialized Internet courts. The first such court was opened in Hangzhou in 2017, followed by courts in Beijing and Guangzhou. Internet courts are an important element of China's strategy to digitalize justice, aimed at improving the efficiency and accessibility of the judicial system. Internet courts in China specialize in handling disputes related to e-commerce, copyright, cybercrime and other issues arising in the digital environment. They use online platforms to file claims, hold meetings and enforce decisions, which significantly reduces case time. AI is used to analyze documents, find precedents and even predict solutions.

Chinese courts are actively introducing AI to automate processes such as document analysis, precedent finding and decision forecasting. For example, the Smart Court system helps judges process large amounts of data, which speeds up decision-making. AI is also used to analyze court decisions and identify possible errors. Blockchain technologies are used to ensure transparency and immutability of judicial data. In China, blockchain is used to store electronic evidence, which makes it more reliable and counterfeit. This is particularly important in cases involving intellectual property and commercial disputes.[53]

Chinese courts use Big Data to analyze judicial practice and identify trends. This makes it possible to predict the burden on the courts, optimize the allocation of resources and improve the quality of justice. For example, data on previous cases help

---

[53]Khoroshko I.V. Foreign experience of electronic form of civil proceedings on the example of the Republic of Singapore and the People's Republic of China: history of origin and current state//Person: crime and punishment. 2022. № 2. S. 183-187.

judges to make more informed decisions. China is actively developing electronic courts that allow online meetings. This was especially true in the context of the COVID-19 pandemic, when many lawsuits went digital and remain in it until now. Online platforms also provide citizens with the opportunity to file claims, track the progress of the case and receive advice.

An important element of the methodology is comparative analysis, which reveals both the positive and negative aspects of digitalization of justice in China. For example, "today the development of artificial intelligence is proceeding at such a pace that there is probably no branch of human activity in which it would not be involved." This statement emphasizes the significance and universality of AI in various fields, including the judicial [54]system. In addition, this 6th study draws on empirical evidence from the operation of Internet courts in China. [55] These courts have become an important part of the e-justice system, providing the opportunity to consider cases online. This approach allows not only to speed up the justice process, but also to make it more accessible to citizens, including foreign parties. Thus, the methodology for the study of e-justice in China is based on an integrated approach, which includes an analysis of legislative changes, technical innovations and practical experience in introducing digital technologies into the judicial system, which provides a comprehensive picture of the current state and prospects for the development of e-justice in China.

The digitalization of justice in China is a complex process that requires careful legal regulation. In recent years, China has been actively introducing information technology into the judicial system, which contributes to improving the efficiency and transparency of judicial processes. The basis of the regulatory framework of digital justice is made up of various regulations and decisions, such as the regulations of the

[54]Kurlyshev A.O. Digitalization and artificial intelligence in criminal proceedings: problems and challenges//Public service and personnel. 2024. № 1. S. 295-298.
[55]Yuwen Li, The Judicial System and Reform in Post-Mao China: Stumbling Towards Justice (The Rule of Law in China and Comparative Perspectives) Routledge Press, 2014, Chapter 5, p. 239.

Supreme People's Court of China on some issues of audio and video recording of court hearings.[56]

One of the key aspects of digitalization is the use of Internet courts, which allow for online court hearings. This innovation greatly simplifies access to justice, especially for residents of remote regions. An important milestone in the development of e-justice was the creation of a pilot Internet court in Zhejiang Province, which dealt with cases related to online payments and copyright infringement on the Internet. In addition, China is actively developing the concept of a "smart court," based on the integration of artificial intelligence in litigation. Such systems are able to analyze large amounts of data and provide the judge with recommendations, which contributes to more objective and fair decision-making. In some courts of the PRC, artificial intelligence has already replaced part of the human workforce, performing the functions of decrypting audio recordings and providing evidence in digital form. [57]Thus, the legislative aspects of digitalization of justice in China are aimed at creating a more efficient and accessible judicial system, which ultimately contributes to strengthening the rule of law and protecting the rights of citizens.

The practical implementation of e-justice in China demonstrates significant advances in the integration of modern technologies into judicial processes. One of the most striking examples is the use of robot judges, which are actively introduced into the judicial system to improve the efficiency and accuracy of decision-making. These robots are able to analyze large amounts of data and provide recommendations to judges, which contributes to more objective and fair justice.[58]

An important aspect is also the use of Internet courts, which allow for online hearings. This innovation greatly simplifies access to justice, especially for residents

---

[56]Konopiy A.S. Digital Transformation of the State and Law of China//North Caucasus Legal Bulletin. 2021. № 3. S. 72-77.

[57]Khoroshko I.V. Foreign experience of electronic form of civil proceedings on the example of the Republic of Singapore and the People's Republic of China: history of origin and current state//Person: crime and punishment. 2022. № 2. S. 183-187.

[58]Ovsyannikova T.A., Firsova I.A. The main elements of the juvenile justice system in China//MNIZH. 2021. № 10-2 (112). S. 176-178.

of remote regions. In Zhejiang Province, a pilot Internet court was established to hear cases involving online payments and Internet copyright infringement. In addition, China is actively developing the concept of a "smart court," based on the integration of artificial intelligence in litigation. Such systems are able to analyze large amounts of data and provide the judge with recommendations, which contributes to more objective and fair decision-making. In some courts of the PRC, artificial intelligence has already replaced part of the human workforce, performing the functions of decrypting audio recordings and providing evidence in digital form. [59]Thus, the practical implementation of e-justice in China not only enhances the effectiveness of the judicial system, but also contributes to strengthening the rule of law and protecting the rights of citizens. The introduction of technologies such as robot judges and Internet courts opens up new prospects for the development of justice in the digital age.[60]

Electronic justice in China offers significant prospects for respecting human rights and freedoms, but it also faces a number of challenges. One of the key benefits is the increased availability of justice, especially for residents of remote regions, through online courts and online meetings. This contributes to faster and more efficient handling of cases, which in turn strengthens citizens' confidence in the judicial system. However, litigation automation raises issues related to data protection and ethics. The introduction of artificial intelligence in lawsuits can lead to risks of violating the confidentiality and security of personal information. As A.O. Kurlyshev notes, "today the development of artificial intelligence is proceeding at such a pace that there is probably no branch of human activity in which it would not be involved." [61]This highlights the need to develop robust data protection mechanisms in a digitalized justice environment.[62]

---

[59]Khoroshko I.V. Foreign experience of electronic form of civil proceedings on the example of the Republic of Singapore and the People's Republic of China: history of origin and current state//Person: crime and punishment. 2022. № 2. S. 183-187.

[60]Zhang, H. (2023). "Smart Courts and the Future of Justice in China". *Asian Journal of Legal Studies*.

[61]Kurlyshev A.O. Digitalization and artificial intelligence in criminal proceedings: problems and challenges//Public service and personnel. 2024. № 1. S. 295-298.

[62]Konopiy A.S. Digital Transformation of the State and Law of China//North Caucasus Legal Bulletin. 2021. № 3. S. 72-77.

Ethical issues also play an important role in the context of the use of robot judges. There is a need to ensure transparency of the algorithms used in court decisions in order to avoid bias and discrimination. It is important that automated systems do not replace the human factor, but only complement it, providing more objective and fair justice. Thus, the prospects for e-justice in China relate to its ability to improve access to justice and trial efficiency. However, the challenges associated with data protection and the ethical aspects of automation must be addressed and overcome to successfully realize these opportunities.[63]

The introduction of digital technologies into the judicial system requires a high level of protection of personal data. In China, where there is strict control over information, it is important to strike a balance between transparency and confidentiality. The use of AI in justice raises questions about the fairness and objectivity of decisions. Algorithms can be prone to error or bias, which can lead to unfair decisions. It is necessary to develop mechanisms for monitoring the work of AI. Not all citizens have equal access to digital technologies, which can create inequalities in access to justice. This is especially true for rural areas and older people who may have difficulty using online platforms.[64]

A study on e-justice in China revealed significant advances in the integration of modern technologies into judicial processes. An important contribution to the study of this problem was the study of A.O. Kurlyshev, who noted that the development of artificial intelligence covers all areas of human activity, including judicial. [65]The significance of the findings lies in the fact that they highlight the potential of digital technologies in improving China's legal system. The introduction of Internet courts and robot judges opens up new opportunities for more objective and fair justice. However,

---

[63]Johnson, R. (2021). "Internet Courts and the Future of Justice: A Global Perspective". *Harvard Journal of Law & Technology*.
[64]Dragilev E.V., Dragileva L.L., Drovaleva L.S., Palamarchuk S.A. Informatization of the judicial system of China//Legal science. 2022. № 8. S. 54-59.
[65]Kurlyshev A.O. Digitalization and artificial intelligence in criminal proceedings: problems and challenges//Public service and personnel. 2024. № 1. S. 295-298.

as A.S. Konopiy notes, it is also necessary to take into account the challenges associated with data protection and ethical aspects of automation.[66]

The digitalization of justice in China is an important step in modernizing the judicial system. It increases the efficiency, transparency and accessibility of justice, but also poses new challenges related to data protection, ethics and equality of access. Successful implementation of digital technologies requires an integrated approach, including legal regulation, technical development and training of citizens. For example, the Smart Court system helps judges process large amounts of data. Blockchain technology is used to store electronic evidence, which ensures its invariability and transparency. Videoconferencing allows participants to participate in meetings from anywhere in the world.

The use of online platforms and the storage of data in digital format create risks of information leakage. In China, where there is strict control over the Internet, privacy issues remain relevant. Automation of trials raises concerns about the fairness of decisions. AI algorithms can be prone to error or bias, which requires the development of controls. Internet courts in China represent an important step in the digitalization of justice. They demonstrate how technology can improve the efficiency and accessibility of the judicial system, but also pose new challenges related to data protection and ethics. China's experience could be useful for other countries seeking to modernize their judicial systems.

2.2. Pre-trial mediation as an important part of pre-trial dispute resolution in China

In China, pre-trial mediation (*sü qián tiáojithe*) since 2012 has been an important part of the alternative dispute resolution (ADR) system and is actively encouraged by

[66]Konopiy A.S. Digital Transformation of the State and Law of China//North Caucasus Legal Bulletin. 2021. № 3. S. 72-77.

the state to reduce the burden on courts and maintain social harmony. Pre-trial mediation in China is regulated by the Constitution of the PRC [1], the Law on Mediation of the PRC (2021), the Civil Procedure Code of the PRC and local regulations. Types of pre-trial mediation:

Popular mediation - *through committees of local residents.*

Judicial mediation - is carried out at the courts, but before the formal adoption of the claim.

Commercial/professional mediation - through specialized centers (for example, at chambers of commerce).

Online mediation - since 2017, platforms such *as* "ODR" (Online Dispute Resolution) have been developing.

Let's consider these types of mediation in more detail.

Popular mediation in China is an extrajudicial dispute settlement mechanism in China based on reconciliation of the parties with the participation of neutral mediators. This institution is part of the system of "social management," aimed at reducing the burden on the courts and maintaining social stability. Popular mediation is carried out on the basis of the principles of voluntary (participation of the parties is based on consent), free of charge (it is important that mediation does not require payment, which ensures its availability for the vast majority of the population in the PRC), flexibility (the procedure is less formal than judicial) and social orientation (justice). Committees of popular mediation are created under: local administrations (urban, rural); enterprises; non-governmental organizations. They include representatives of local authorities, respected community members (elders, veterans), as well as lawyers and activists.[67]

---

[67]Grudtsyna L.Y. Electronic Justice in China//International Scientific Bulletin. 2025. № 2. P. 28.

The legal basis of popular mediation is:

- *The Law "On Popular Mediation"* (2010, as amended in 2021) is the main normative act.[68]
- *Regulations on popular mediation committees* - regulate the activities of mediators.
- *The Civil Procedure Code of the PRC* - recognizes mediation agreements that have the force of court decisions after their certification by the court.

The procedure of popular mediation consists of 5 stages, including: filing an application - one of the parties applies to the committee; choosing a mediator - the parties can agree on a candidate; negotiations - mediator listens to positions, offers solutions; conclusion of an agreement - upon successful settlement; certification in court (if necessary) - to make the agreement binding. With the help of traditional mediation in China, family disputes (divorces, inheritance), neighboring conflicts (land issues, noise), as well as labor disputes can be resolved.

It is important to note that since 2010, the use of popular mediation, firstly, reduces the burden on the courts - up to 75% of disputes are resolved through mediation, secondly, it supports social stability - it prevents the escalation of conflicts, and combined with the "socialist rule of law," reflects the Chinese model of "virtue rule." Popular mediation in China is an important tool for maintaining social order, combining the traditional values of Confucian reconciliation with modern legal mechanisms. Despite its shortcomings, the system remains a key element of China's dispute resolution model.[69]

Judicial mediation in China is a dispute resolution procedure involving a court, where a judge or authorized mediator helps the parties reach a voluntary agreement.

---

[68]PRC. Laws. Civil Procedure Code: Law of the People's Republic of China: [adopted on April 9, 1991: as amended on November 28, 2007]. - URL: https://chinalawinfo.ru/procedural_law/law_civil_procedure (date of access: 04.05.2025).
[69]Kalashnikova S.I. Mediation in the field of civil jurisdiction/S.I. Kalashnikova - M.: InfotropicMedia, 2011. — 304 c.

Unlike traditional mediation, judicial mediation is integrated into the judicial process and can be applied at any stage of the case.

The key features of this type of mediation are the following: the mediation procedure is carried out under the control of the court (but not always by the judge himself); it combines elements of mediation and litigation; the agreement has the force of judgment after approval by the court; applied in civil, commercial, family and some administrative disputes.

Forms of judicial mediation in China are: *mediation conducted by a judge* - the judge acts as an intermediary before or during a court session; *mediation with the involvement of external specialists* (the court delegates the procedure to professional mediators or people's mediation committees), *online mediation* - through specialized platforms (for example, "Smart Court").

The stages of judicial mediation in China are classified into:

Initiation - the court offers mediation, the parties may agree or refuse.

Choice of mediator - judge, external expert or collegial body.

Negotiations - possible compromises are discussed.

Conclusion of an agreement - if the parties come to a consensus.

Court approval - the agreement acquires the force of a court decision.

The areas of application of judicial mediation are, first of all, civil and commercial disputes (debts, contracts, property), family conflicts (divorces, custody of children), labor disputes, as well as minor criminal cases (reconciliation in cases of private prosecution).[70]

---

[70]Grudtsyna L.Y. Issues of the organization of electronic justice in the European Union//Research Institute for Education and Law. 2025. № 1-3. S. 14-18.

The advantages of judicial mediation are: a) speed - allows you to resolve the dispute faster than a regular lawsuit, b) flexibility - the parties can offer non-standard solutions, c) reducing conflict - mediation helps to preserve relations, d) mandatory force of the agreement - after approval by the court it is subject to enforcement. However, China still lacks qualified mediators (especially in the Chinese provinces), as well as the unresolved problem is the limited transparency of this procedure (for example, some decisions are made without sufficient public control).[71]

Judicial mediation in China is an important element of the legal system, combining the flexibility of out-of-court settlement with the legal force of a court decision. It complements popular mediation, providing greater opportunities for conflict resolution. Despite some problems, this institution continues to develop, reflecting China's general course towards harmonizing society and reducing the judicial burden.

Commercial (professional) mediation in China is a specialized mechanism for out-of-court settlement of disputes between enterprises, entrepreneurs and other participants in commercial activities with the involvement of professional mediators.

The key features of this type of mediation are as follows:

Voluntary - the parties themselves choose the mediator and the conditions of the procedure.

Confidentiality - the process and results are not disclosed without the consent of the parties.

Professionalism - mediators have legal or business education and experience in commercial disputes.

Flexibility - the parties can agree on non-standard settlement terms.

---

[71] Grudtsyna L.Y. Electronic Justice in China//International Scientific Bulletin. 2025. № 2. P. 28.

The legal basis for the application of commercial (professional) mediation in China is:

The Law of the PRC "On Mediation" (2010, as amended in 2021) - regulates the general principles of mediation, including commercial.

Rules of the Supreme People's Court on Mediation (2021) - clarify the application of mediation in commercial disputes.

International standards - China recognizes the UN Singapore Convention on Mediation Agreements (2020), which simplifies the implementation of international mediation decisions.

Types of commercial mediation are: internal commercial mediation - disputes between Chinese companies, international commercial mediation - disputes involving foreign enterprises, industry mediation - specialized centers (for example, for IT, construction, finance).[72]

The main institutions for the implementation of commercial mediation are:

China Center for International Commercial Media (CICMC) as a key government platform.

Shanghai International Mediation Center (SCIMC), which specializes in free trade zone disputes.

Private mediation centers (for example, at the China Arbitration Commission, CIETAC).

The commercial mediation procedure consists of five stages: 1) conclusion of a mediation agreement - the parties agree on the rules; 2) selection of a mediator - from the list of accredited specialists; 3) negotiation - mediator helps to find a compromise;

[72]Korosteleva Yu.A., Simonovsky D.A. Legal regulation of mediation in China: a brief review//International research journal. 2023. № 6 (132). P. 12.

4) signing of the agreement - if the parties come to a consensus; 5) execution - voluntary or through court/arbitration (if necessary). It is important to note that in recent years, important trends have emerged in China, including: digitalization (online mediation through Smart Court platforms), the development of international mediation (China promotes its centers as an alternative to Western ones) and cooperation with Hong Kong and Singapore (creation of cross-border dispute settlement mechanisms).

Let's compare commercial (professional) mediation with other types of mediation in China (Table 1).

Table 1. Comparison of commercial (professional) with other types mediation in China.

Criterion	**Commercial Mediation**	**Folk mediation**	**Judicial mediation**
Participants	Business, entrepreneurs	Individuals, local disputes	Any parties to the litigation
Mediators	Professionals (lawyers, experts)	Social activists, elders	Judges or invited mediators
Cost	Paid (but cheaper than the court)	Free	Free or low cost
Power of Agreement	Can be approved by court/arbitration	Requires certification in court	Has the force of a court decision

Thus, it can be concluded that commercial mediation in China is a promising tool for business, especially in the face of growing international transactions. It offers a balance between flexibility and legal protection, but requires further infrastructure development and increased business confidence. The state actively supports this institution, which makes it an important part of the Chinese alternative dispute resolution (ADR) system.

Online mediation in China is an electronic procedure for resolving conflicts through Internet platforms using video communication, chats and digital documents. The legal basis of this type of mediation is:

The Law "On Mediation" (2010, as amended in 2021) - allows remote procedures.

Directive of the Supreme People's Court (2021) - regulates online mediation in the judicial system.

Cybersecurity and data protection regulations - ensure confidentiality.

The key platforms for online mediation are **Smart Court** as the official system of courts of the PRC (integration with judicial mediation, as well as the ability to file applications and sign agreements with EDS); **Commercial mediation centre platforms** (e.g. China International Commercial Court (CICC) for cross-border disputes; private services (e.g. Alibaba Mediation Center for e-commerce); **WeChat mediation** (through mini-programs in WeChat (e.g., "Judicial WeChat" in Guangdong). The areas of application of online mediation are: commercial disputes (contracts, deliveries), consumer complaints (especially in e-commerce), various family and labor conflicts, as well as international disputes (involving foreign companies).

The procedure for online mediation in China consists of several stages: 1) filing an application through an electronic system; 2) verification of the parties by ID or business registration; 3) selection of a mediator from the accredited list; 4) sessions in Zoom/WeMeeting with recording (by agreement of the parties); 5) electronic signing of the agreement with legal force.[73]

The advantages of online mediation, in our opinion, are: firstly, its availability (the ability to participate in online mediation procedures from anywhere in the world), secondly, speed - the average dispute resolution period is now 7-14 days in China, thirdly, cost reduction (there is no need for face-to-face meetings), fourthly, state support (integration with "digital vessels"). But, at the same time, in addition to the

---

Danshin A.V. Institute of Mediation in Traditional China (X-XIX centuries) ./A.V. Danshin//Historical, philosophical, political and legal sciences, cultural studies and art [73]history. Questions of theory and practice. — 2014. — 12 (50). — c. 42-46.

advantages, there are certain problems for the development of online mediation procedures in China, for example, technical barriers - stable Internet is required, trust in the procedure - some participants prefer the face-to-face format, cybersecurity issues - the risks of data leaks. Development trends in the coming years will be: AI mediation - algorithms for primary analysis of disputes are being tested; blockchain for agreements - for example, the Hangzhou Internet Court platform; expanding to international disputes - synchronizing with the UN Singapore Convention. Compare online mediation with offline mediation in Table 2.

Table 2. Comparison of online mediation with traditional (offline) mediation in China.

Criterion	Online mediation	Offline Mediation
Terms	1-3 weeks	1-6 months
Cost	30-50% cheaper	Above (logistics, rental of halls)
Geography	Unlimited	Local Format
Flexibility	24/7 access to materials	Fixed Schedule

Based on the above, we draw the following conclusions.

Firstly, China is actively leading in the digitalization of mediation, making it the main tool for business and citizens. The online format combines the effectiveness of traditional methods with technological advantages, although it requires improvement in terms of security and trust. In the coming years, we should expect further growth in this segment, especially in international disputes.[74]

Secondly, the essence of the pre-trial mediation procedure is that the parties can apply to the mediation body before filing a lawsuit. [75]If an agreement is reached, it can be certified by the court and obtain the force of the writ of execution. If mediation fails, the case is brought to court. The advantages of this type of mediation are: speed (mediation time is usually 15-30 days), savings on court costs, flexibility and confidentiality. In some regions of China, up to 40-60% of civil disputes are resolved

[74]Grudtsyna L.Y. Electronic Justice in China//International Scientific Bulletin. 2025. № 2. P. 28.
[75]Grudtsyna L.Y. Digitalization of Justice in the USA: Case Management Electronic Case Files (CMECF) and Public Access to Court Electronic Records (PACER)//Law and Management. 2025. № 2. S. 114.

through pre-trial mediation. Chinese courts actively direct cases to mediation through "multi-stage dispute resolution" systems.

Thirdly, commercial mediation in China is a promising tool for business, especially in the face of growing international transactions. It offers a balance between flexibility and legal protection, but requires further infrastructure development and increased business confidence. The state actively supports this institution, which makes it an important part of the Chinese alternative dispute resolution (ADR) system.

CHAPTER 3.

E-JUSTICE IN COUNTRIES EUROPEAN UNION

This chapter is devoted to the study of e-justice in some countries of the European Union (Germany, France, Spain, Latvia, Lithuania, Estonia and Romania). The national legal regulation of the digitalization of legal proceedings is considered, examples of the transition of the judicial systems of these countries to electronic forms are analyzed, and the challenges and effectiveness of such transformations in the aspect of a single legal space of the European Union are assessed.

3.1. GENERAL PROVISIONS ON DIGITAL JUSTICE IN THE EUROPEAN UNION

E-justice in the countries of the European Union is a relevant and significant topic in the context of the modern development of the legal system. The digitalization of trials contributes to improving the efficiency and accessibility of justice, which is especially important in the context of globalization and an increase in the volume of court cases. However, despite the obvious advantages, the process of introducing e-justice is accompanied by a number of contradictions and challenges. One of the key contradictions is the need to ensure data protection and privacy in the context of digitalization. The introduction of electronic systems requires the creation of reliable mechanisms for protecting information, which becomes especially relevant in the light of growing cybersecurity threats. In addition, there is a problem of unequal access to electronic resources among citizens, which can lead to discrimination and violation of the principle of equality before the law.[76]

The legal and ethical issues associated with the use of robot judges also generate considerable debate. As E.B. Ablaeva notes, "the rule of law, at the same time, imposes requirements related to the content of adopted laws - laws must be legal; to the activities of the judiciary - the courts must be independent and administer fair justice." [77]This emphasizes the need to comply with ethical standards and ensure the independence of the judiciary when introducing artificial intelligence technologies.

The current degree of scientific development of the topic of e-justice in the EU is quite high. V.A. Goshin's studies emphasize the importance of judicial practice in ensuring the uniform application of EU law and the development of general principles of Community law. At the same time, Z.I. Tagirov focuses on the importance of coordinating efforts at the EU level to ensure security and protect the rights of citizens. Thus, the problem that will be addressed in this paragraph of the monograph is to assess the legal regulation and practical implementation of e-justice in the EU, as well as to analyze the prospects for using technology to respect human rights. The study is aimed at identifying optimal strategies and approaches that will ensure effective and fair justice in the context of digitalization.

The methodology for e-justice research in the European Union requires an integrated approach that takes into account both legal and technical aspects. As part of the legal analysis, special attention is paid to the study of EU legislation governing the digitalization of justice. This includes an analysis of directives and regulations aimed

[76]Grudtsyna L.Y. Digitalization of justice in the European Union//International Scientific Bulletin. 2025. № 7. S. 198-204.

[77]E.B. Ablaeva "Rule of law" in the work of international organizations//Gaps in Russian legislation. 2017. №7. P. 199.

at unifying and standardizing electronic litigation. Technical aspects, in turn, focus on the implementation of information systems that automate judicial procedures and access to justice through digital platforms.[78]

The social and ethical implications of technology in justice are also an important part of the study. In this context, the protection of human rights and justice in the context of the automation of judicial decisions are considered. As V.A. Goshin notes, "court decisions ensure the interpretation and uniform application of EU law, the development of the so-called general principles of Community law." [79]This highlights the importance of judicial practice in the context of the digitalization of justice.

Research methods include a comparative analysis of the legal systems of different EU countries, which reveals general trends and differences in approaches to e-justice. In addition, empirical methods are used, such as surveys and interviews with experts in the field of law and information technology, which contributes to a better understanding of the practical aspects of introducing electronic systems into judicial practice. Thus, an integrated approach to the study of e-justice in the EU allows not only to assess the current state, but also to determine the prospects for its development in the context of digital transformation.

In recent years, the European Union has been actively promoting the digitalization of justice, which is reflected in the adoption of a number of directives and regulations aimed at introducing electronic forms of justice. One of the key documents in this area is Regulation (EU) 2018/1724, which establishes uniform standards for the provision of administrative services in digital format. This regulation contributes to the unification of approaches to e-justice among EU member states, providing more effective and accessible justice for citizens. The implementation of these regulations in the national legislation of the EU member states varies depending on the level of readiness and technical equipment of each country. For example, Germany and France

---

[78]Grudtsyna L.Y. Digitalization of justice in the European Union//International Scientific Bulletin. 2025. № 7. S. 198-204.

[79]Goshin V.A. Judicial precedent as a source of European Union law//Gaps in Russian legislation. 2015. №4. S. 294.

have already made significant progress in integrating electronic systems into judicial processes, thus speeding up cases and reducing administrative costs. At the same time, in some countries, such as the Czech Republic and Italy, the process of implementing e-justice faces certain difficulties related to the need to modernize infrastructure and train staff.[80]

Judicial practice also plays an important role in the development of e-justice in the EU. As V. A. Goshin notes, "the provisions of judicial practice developed on the basis of these norms contain an interpretation and a kind of generalizing experience and recommendations for their practical application." [81]This underlines the importance of judicial decisions in ensuring the uniform application of EU law and the development of general principles of Community law. Thus, the legal regulation of e-justice in the European Union is a complex and multifaceted process that requires coordination between the EU and national governments. The introduction of electronic forms of justice helps not only to increase the effectiveness of the judicial system, but also to strengthen citizens' confidence in justice, which is an important step towards the development of European democracy.[82]

The practical implementation of e-justice in the countries of the European Union demonstrates a variety of approaches and strategies based on national characteristics and technological readiness. Germany and France are examples of countries where the digitalization of litigation has achieved significant success. In Germany, for example, the introduction of electronic systems made it possible to optimize the process of filing and processing documents, which significantly reduced the time of consideration of cases. France is also actively using electronic platforms for interaction between courts

---

[80]Grudtsyna L.Y. Digitalization of legal proceedings on the example of some countries of the European Union//Academic Science. 2025. № 1. S. 65-72.

[81]Goshin V.A. Judicial precedent as a source of European Union law//Gaps in Russian legislation. 2015. №4. S. 290.

[82]Grudtsyna L.Y. Issues of the organization of electronic justice in the European Union//Research Institute for Education and Law. 2025. № 1-3. S. 14-18.

and participants in the process, which contributes to the transparency and accessibility of justice.[83]

At the same time, in the Czech Republic and Italy, the process of transition to electronic forms of justice is facing certain challenges. In the Czech Republic, the main obstacles are insufficient modernization of infrastructure and the need to train judicial personnel in new technologies. Italy, in turn, faces problems of integrating different information systems, which requires considerable investment and coordination at the level of public authorities.[84]

Spain, like other EU countries, is actively working to introduce electronic systems into litigation. However, as Z.I. Tagirov notes, "by providing information exchange, the justice and internal affairs system contributes to the implementation of a unified political course in countering terrorism." [85] This highlights the importance of coordinating efforts at EU level to ensure security and protect the rights of citizens. Thus, the practical implementation of e-justice in EU countries is a complex and multifaceted process that requires taking into account national characteristics and coordination at the European Union level. Despite the existing challenges, the digitalization of justice opens up new opportunities for improving the efficiency and accessibility of the judicial system, which helps to strengthen citizens' confidence in justice and the development of European democracy.[86]

In recent years, the European Union has been actively introducing artificial intelligence technologies into litigation, which opens up new horizons for justice. One of the most discussed aspects is the use of robot judges who can perform functions traditionally assigned to humans. Examples of such technologies can already be

---

[83]Sutormina L.A. Readmission as an instrument of the immigration policy of the European Union (on the example of the readmission agreement with Russia)//Bulletin of Moscow University. Series 25. International relations and world politics. 2011. №1. S. 149-162.

[84]Grudtsyna L.Y. Judicial precedent and judicial law-making: public-legal aspect//Education and law. 2024. № 8. S. 98-103.

[85]Tagirov Z.I. Modern activities of the police of the European Union to counter terrorism//Bulletin of the Kazan Law Institute of the Ministry of Internal Affairs of Russia. 2019. №4 (38). S. 426-430.

[86]Malko A.V., Elistratova V.V. Problems of the formation of the judicial system of the Eurasian Economic Union//Socio-political sciences. 2017. №3. S. 43-47.

observed in some EU countries, where they are used to automate routine tasks, such as document processing and precedent analysis.

The prospects for the use of robot judges in the EU are related to the possibility of increasing the efficiency of the judicial system and reducing the time of consideration of cases. However, as E.B. Ablaeva notes, "the rule of law, at the same time, imposes requirements related to the content of the adopted laws - the laws must be legal; to the activities of the judiciary - the courts must be independent and administer fair justice." [87]This underlines the need to comply with ethical and legal standards when introducing such technologies.

The ethical aspects of the use of robot judges cause considerable debate. The main concerns are related to the possibility of violation of human rights and freedoms, as well as issues of responsibility for decisions made by artificial intelligence. It is important that the introduction of such technologies does not undermine the confidence of citizens in the judicial system and does not violate the principles of justice and equality.

In the context of the development of European democracy, robot judges can play a significant role in providing more transparent and accessible justice. However, this requires the development of a clear legal framework that will regulate their use and guarantee the protection of citizens' rights. [88]Thus, the integration of robot judges into the EU judicial system requires a balanced approach, taking into account both technological capabilities and legal and ethical standards. A study on e-justice in the European Union identified significant achievements and challenges related to the digitalization of trials. The authors of the article, such as V.A. Goshin and E.B. Ablaeva, made a significant contribution to the analysis of legal regulation and

---

[87]E.B. Ablaeva "Rule of law" in the work of international organizations//Gaps in Russian legislation. 2017. №7. P. 199.
[88]Grudtsyna L.Y. Digitalization of legal proceedings on the example of some countries of the European Union//Academic Science. 2025. № 1. S. 65-72.

practical implementation of electronic justice, emphasizing the importance of unifying approaches and compliance with legal norms.

The obtained results emphasize the importance of the introduction of electronic systems to increase the efficiency and accessibility of justice, which helps to strengthen the confidence of citizens in the judicial system. The introduction of artificial intelligence technologies, such as robot judges, opens up new prospects for automating routine tasks, but requires careful observance of ethical and legal norms so as not to undermine the principles of justice and equality.

3.2. ELECTRONIC JUSTICE IN GERMANY AND FRANCE

In ***Germany*** in 2001, the first electronic document flow appeared, allowing the exchange of documents between all participants in the process. 20 years have passed and since January 1, 2022, for lawyers, authorities and legal entities, the exchange of procedural documents with courts in Germany is possible only in electronic form. Paper claims and complaints are no longer accepted (with rare exceptions).

The German Civil Procedure Code (adopted in 1887) contains codified rules on the digitalization of the civil process. Consider its key paragraphs.

§ 128a - video session. The court may hold a meeting with the participation of the parties by audio and video communication; Since 19.07.2024, the participation of witnesses/experts and a parallel broadcast to the courtroom have been clarified.

§ 130a - electronic document. Procedural documents are submitted as electronic documents (in a digital image) suitable for processing by a court; either with a qualified electronic signature or through a "secure communication channel."

§ 130d - electronic filing duty. For lawyers and public authorities, electronic filing is mandatory; rare exceptions are allowed if there is no technical possibility to submit documents electronically (but there are practically no such cases). Since 2025, the obligation of electronic filing extends to lawyers from other EU countries, acting, conducting cases of their clients in courts in Germany.

§ 130e - "form fiction." Short story 2024: if the required "written" will is clearly contained in the application filed as an electronic document, it is considered to comply with the written/electronic form.

§ 173-174 - electronic delivery rule. Electronic delivery is allowed only through a "safe communication channel"; proof is "electronic acknowledgement of receipt" in machine-readable form.

§ 298a - electronic court case. Electronic case management from January 1, 2026 is a general rule; the technical organization of electronic litigation is determined by the by-laws of the lands.

§ 299 - familiarization with the case. For electronic cases, the "digital-first" approach applies: access is provided through a portal or a secure channel; paper printouts are provided in exceptional cases.

For authorities and other participants, a special system of interdepartmental interaction EGVP (Elektronisches Gerichts- und Verwaltungspostfach) is provided. It works on a similar principle, allowing the exchange of documents between the courts, the prosecutor's office and state bodies. The most important tool for the functioning of electronic justice in Germany is the **Electronic Court and Administrative Mailbox** (EGVP). This is a special secure electronic lawyer's box through which lawyers are required to interact with the courts. Access strictly by qualified electronic signature (lawyer card). Data transmission is encrypted and meets high security standards.[89]

To use this system, the user must install a special program "Electronic judicial and administrative mailbox" on his computer. The program is free and available for

[89]Grudtsyna L.Y. Predictive proceedings: comparative analysis of law enforcement practice in the USA, Germany, France and China//International Scientific Bulletin. 2025. № 4. S. 162-167.

installation on official sites. The programme was the result of successful administrative reform and promotes the implementation of new provisions of German e-justice legislation. According to German law, scientific and technical means of communication must ensure an effective document flow of legal information between the population and the state apparatus.

The electronic judicial and administrative mailbox provides users with such opportunities as round-the-clock access to information judicial resources, reliable data transmission, secure communication using cryptographic mechanisms, the ability to electronically process files, receive automatic notifications by e-mail, and support for all accredited signature cards. In practice, the Electronic Court and Administrative Mailbox system in Germany works as follows:

1) Filing of claims, complaints and applications is carried out online, directly to the court.

2) Court decisions are also sent to the parties through electronic boxes.

3) Minutes of meetings can be recorded and stored digitally.

4) Participants in the process have access to the case in electronic format, which speeds up communication.

The websites of the courts of Germany have all the necessary information that helps the user to familiarize themselves with the rules of procedure in each of them. Court decisions are also published on official websites and are accessible to a wide range of people.

It is important to note that Germany, practicing electronic legal resources, aims, first of all, to make justice accessible to the whole population and to everyone. For example, on the websites of courts and other legal sites, the information provided is not presented in a complex "legal" language, but in a simple accessible language.[90]

In addition, the sites contain special information for people with disabilities. An analysis of electronic justice services in Germany suggests that its main achievement is electronic document management. Germany also pays special attention to the issue of ensuring safe and confidential document flow. Reforms in the field of electronic justice in Germany have the priority goal of introducing additional security protocols into it and do not imply saturation with the new electronic justice services widely used in a number of other countries.

Germany has a ban on automated decision forecasting (BVerfG, 2019). The German Federal Constitutional Court has banned the use of a system that predicts the likelihood of a crime based on police data (similar to predictive policing). The algorithm used historical data, which could increase discrimination against minorities. [91]The court ruled that such systems violate the principle of individual case management (Art. 103 GG) and Personal Data Protection (GDPR). In Germany, predictive systems in criminal law are limited due to strict privacy requirements and the inadmissibility of algorithmic discrimination.

Over the past decade, ***France has carried out a reform of the digital transformation of justice: open data of court decisions, mandatory and voluntary electronic channels for different jurisdictions, regulation of the interaction of professional participants (lawyers, administrations) with the courts.***

The reform of the digital transformation of French justice began with the "Digital Republic Law" of 2016, after which the French Ministry of Justice formed a roadmap for the phased publication of decisions of administrative and judicial jurisdictions.

---

[90]Grudtsyna L.Y. Issues of the organization of electronic justice in the European Union//Research Institute for Education and Law. 2025. № 1-3. S. 14-18.
[91]BVerfG, Urteil vom 15.12.2019 – 1 BvR 2765/16.

For professional participants (administrations, lawyers), electronic exchange in administrative cases is carried out through a special portal and the e-Barreau web interface; there is a separate portal for citizens. Portals provide filing, document exchange, notification, and case status tracking. In 2025, integration with the law firms "e-Barreau web interface was implemented.

In administrative cases, lawyers submit documents through the special portal Télérecours; the system assigns a number and generates a confirmation/receipt. To comply with the submission of procedural documents, the date of electronic deposit recorded by the system is relevant.

In civil/commercial cases, lawyers can also file procedural acts (for example, declaration of appeal, written explanations, evidence) based on the rules of electronic exchange of CPC; in this case, confirmations and notifications are delivered to the "mailbox" of the system, and the lawyer is notified of this. It is important to understand here that electronic communication and electronic filing do not cancel the procedural requirements for appearance and form, unless otherwise expressly provided by French law.

Consider the two main documents regulating the digitalization of trials in France, these are the Code of Civil Procedure of France in 1976 (as amended and supplemented) and the French Code of Judicial Organization in 1978.

To understand the structure of the French GPC, it is important to note that digitalization in the GPC is based on fundamental principles from the Civil Code (Code civil), such as articles 1316-1 to 1316-4, which equate electronic documents and signatures to their paper counterparts, subject to the criteria of identification, integrity and immutability.

However, the GPK adapts this to procedural contexts, emphasizing practical implementation in court conditions for specific court cases. For example, electronic acts are seen as equivalents to traditional ones, allowing systems such as the e-Barreau platform - a virtual network connecting attorneys and courts (via RPVJ) - to facilitate electronic filing, document exchange, and case tracking. This system was first launched in 2003 in Paris and implemented nationally in 2005.

Thus, the French Code of Civil Procedure (Code de procédure civile, CPC) [92](hereinafter referred to as the French CPC) has gradually integrated digital tools for modernizing civil justice, focusing on electronic communications as a fundamental element. Introduced by Decree No. 2005-1678 of 28 December 2005

Section XXI covers articles 748-1 to 748-9 and establishes rules for electronic dispatch, notifications and acts, emphasizing consent, security and reliability.

Consider specific articles. You see them in the presentation. Let's dwell on two articles.

Art. 748-1 The French Code of Civil Procedure allows electronic methods of dispatch, delivery and electronic notifications of procedural acts.

Article 748-3 of the French Code of Civil Procedure provides for two mechanisms for recording the receipt of procedural documents online: electronic or so-called electronic "notice of placement" to the selected address; both options specify the date and time and replace the stamps and signatures provided for the paper exchange. The court may require the original document in court if the document was originally on paper.

The French Judicial Code of 1978 is a codified law that establishes how civil and criminal courts are organized and function in France. The Code does not regulate independent administrative courts (they have their own Code - Code de justice administrative) and does not replace procedural rules (they are established by the Code

[92]Additional information on the New French Code of Civil Procedure and the French Code of Civil Procedure of 1806 see Reference dictionary of basic terms in the following publication: *French Commercial Code*. (Preface, translation, supplement, reference apparatus and comments by V. N. Zakhvataev). - Volters Kluver, M. 2008. - P. 755-756; 856—857.

of Civil Procedure and the Code of Criminal Procedure of France. The French Judicial Code defines the "skeleton" of the judicial system and its services.

The French Judicial Code regulates:

- structure and levels of judicial courts, their territorial organization, names and locations;
- Composition of judicial boards and forms of work of chambers/departments;
- work of offices, basic standards of publicity of meetings;
- Certain "digital" provisions: for example, the possibility of audio-visual communication meetings, conditions and restrictions on the electronic publication of court decisions;
- Distribution of managerial powers of court presidents and first presidents of appeals, as well as the French Court of Cassation in matters of organization of work.

France does not have a single (one) digital platform dedicated to justice and justice. There are several platforms. For example, the Tribunal Digital platform (launched in 2019) is only for commercial disputes, there is also a justice.fr platform for family disputes, allowing citizens to initiate processes online, with safe online.

The French model demonstrates the so-called "dynamic equilibrium." On the one hand, large-scale digitalization of open data channels and systems increases access to justice, reduces transaction costs and supports predictability of procedures (receipts, timestamps, notifications, all this is transparent and visible to judges and participants in the trial). On the other hand, the French legislator creates tough barriers for algorithms that can affect judicial individualization and independence.[93]

France has implemented the Predictice AI platform (2020) to analyze judicial practice and predict decisions in civil cases. [94]Lawyers and judges expressed concerns

---

[93]Grudtsyna L.Y. Digitalization of legal proceedings on the example of some countries of the European Union//Academic Science. 2025. № 1. S. 65-72.
[94]CNIL, "L'IA dans la justice" (2021).

that the system could simplify complex legal issues. The National Commission on Informatics and Freedoms (CNIL) has obliged developers to ensure the transparency of algorithms and the right to explain decisions. Thus, France is carefully introducing predictive technologies, focusing on control by lawyers.

So, we reviewed the legislation and some processes of digitalization of justice in Germany and France. Several conclusions can be drawn.

First, Germany and France are examples of countries where the digitalization of litigation has achieved significant success over the past few years. However, these are not leading countries in the field of digitalization. The leaders in this area are the USA, China and Estonia.

Secondly, in Germany, the introduction of electronic systems made it possible to optimize the process of filing and processing documents, which significantly reduced the time of consideration of cases. France is also actively using electronic platforms for interaction between courts and participants in the process, which contributes to the transparency and accessibility of justice.

Thirdly, there are no "robot judges" in France yet (as of 2025-2026); auxiliary automation with guaranteed judicial independence and procedural rights of the parties is permissible. In France, there is a "combined" model: the active introduction of digital channels and open data with regulatory barriers to individualizing predictive analytics systems.

3.3. E-JUSTICE IN THE KINGDOM OF SPAIN

The digital transformation of the judicial systems of European states is a global trend aimed at improving the efficiency, transparency and accessibility of justice in the European Union. The Kingdom of Spain is actively developing digital technologies in the field of justice, following both European directives and national strategies for modernizing justice. The use of electronic means in litigation in Spain has already yielded significant results, increasing their transparency, accessibility and efficiency.[95]

Key projects and initiatives in the field of digitalization of legal proceedings in Spain:

1. Single digital judicial platform (LexNET 2.0). Modernization of LexNET - the main system of electronic document management. Integration with other state platforms (for example, with the tax service and the property register). Ability to file claims and motions online for citizens and lawyers.

2. Virtual courts and remote meetings. Increased use of videoconferencing (especially after COVID-19 experience). Digital summons and notifications (SMS, e-mail, push notifications).

3. Artificial intelligence and Big Data in justice. Pilot projects on forecasting court decisions (analysis of precedents). Automatic processing of routine requests (e.g. collection of fines).

4. Cybersecurity and data protection (creation of the Center for Cybersecurity of Justice (CERT-Justicia), encryption of personal data in judicial databases).

The legal framework for the digitalization of justice in the Kingdom of Spain includes the following legal acts:

- Law 18/2011 on the Regulation of the Use of Electronic Technologies in Judicial Activities.
- Digital Justice Transformation Plan 2019-2023, approved by the General Council of the Judiciary (CGPJ).

[95]Grudtsyna L.Y. Digitalization of legal proceedings on the example of some countries of the European Union//Academic Science. 2025. № 1. S. 65-72.

- EU Directives, including the eIDAS (Electronic Identification and Fiduciary Services) Regulation.[96]

These documents fix the transition to electronic document management, digital signature and remote participation in litigation. Let's look at them in more detail.

Spanish Law 18/2011 of July 5 on the Regulation of the Use of Electronic Technologies in Judicial Activities (*Ley reguladora del uso de las tecnologías de la información y la comunicación en la Administración de Justicia*) is the key regulation that laid the foundations for the digitalization of the Spanish judicial system. Its main goal is to modernize justice through the introduction of electronic technologies, ensuring the efficiency, transparency and accessibility of judicial procedures.

Court documents may be filed electronically through specialized platforms (e.g. LexNET). Electronic signatures (including those qualified under the eIDAS Regulation) are recognized as legally significant. In addition, the exchange of documents between the courts, the prosecutor's office and the participants in the process is simplified. Traditional paper notifications are replaced by electronic notifications (via portals, SMS or e-mail). The presumption of delivery is established - if the message is sent through the official system, it is considered received. The law allows for virtual meetings using videoconferencing, especially for: interrogations of witnesses and experts, as well as the participation of parties located abroad. Electronic registers of court decisions are created (in compliance with the protection of personal data). Citizens and lawyers can request information online.

The Spanish law 18/2011 is of great importance for the digitalization of justice: firstly, with its adoption and implementation, there was an acceleration of judicial procedures (reducing the time for consideration of cases due to automation), secondly, the implementation of this law has reduced the bureaucratic burden on courts (for example, reducing dependence on paper carriers), thirdly, Spanish Law 18/2011

---

[96]Grudtsyna L.Y. Digitalization of justice in the kingdom of Spain//Humanities. High School. 2025. № 2. S. 35-40.

complies with EU standards, in particular, the Directive on electronic justice (2020/1828). Spanish [97] Law 18/2011 became the basis for subsequent reforms, including the 2019-2023 Digital Justice Transformation Plan. In the future, it is expected: wider use of artificial intelligence (for example, for analyzing judicial practice), as well as integration with European digital systems (for example, e-CODEX for cross-border cases). Thus, it can be concluded that Law 18/2011 has established Spain among the leaders in the digitalization of justice in the EU. However, to fully realize its potential, further technology development and training of process participants are required.[98]

The 2019-2023 Plan for the Digital Transformation of Justice (Plan de Transformación Digital de la Justicia) is a strategic programme developed by the Spanish General Council of the Judiciary (CGPJ) with the support of the Ministry of Justice. Its goal is to modernize the judicial system through the introduction of advanced digital technologies, increasing the efficiency and accessibility of justice. The plan is based on three key principles:

Efficiency - expediting litigation through automation.

Transparency - ensuring the openness of data (taking into account the protection of confidentiality).

Accessibility - simplification of interaction of citizens and lawyers with courts.

Strategic directions: (1) full digitalization of legal proceedings (from filing a lawsuit to execution of a decision), (2) development of electronic justice (Justicia Digital), (3) introduction of artificial intelligence for data analysis and forecasting, (4) strengthening cybersecurity of judicial systems.

---

[97] Ley 18/2011, de 5 de julio, reguladora del uso de las tecnologías de la información y la comunicación en la Administración de Justicia.
[98] Plan de Transformación Digital de la Justicia 2019–2023. CGPJ.

The digitalization of Spanish justice is implemented not only at the legislative level, but also through specific court decisions. Let's consider key cases demonstrating the use of digital technologies in judicial practice.

Case number 1: The first fully digital trial (2020, Audiensia Nacional). The essence of the matter: Consideration of a commercial dispute between the two companies. Digital tools: All documents are submitted via LexNET. Participation of witnesses and experts via videoconferencing. Electronic signing of the court decision. Bottom line: The review time was reduced by 30% compared to the traditional process.

Case number 2: Using AI to predict decisions (2022, Supreme Court of Catalonia). The essence of the case: Analysis of the same type of claims for debt collection. Digital tools: AI algorithm processed 500 + similar cases in 2 days. The system highlighted typical arguments and solutions. Bottom line: Judges used the data to speed up decision-making, reducing review time by 25%.

Case number 3: Blockchain for evidence verification (2021, Madrid Court of Justice). The essence of the matter: The dispute over the authenticity of digital documents. Digital tools: Evidence is recorded in the blockchain (immutable registry). The court verified the authenticity in 5 minutes (usually weeks were required). Bottom line: The first precedent for using blockchain in Spanish justice.

Case number 4: Remote participation of convicts in meetings (2023, Valencia). Point: Prisoner's appeal. Digital tools: The convict participated through a secure video channel from prison. Electronic document exchange with a lawyer. Total: Saving time and money for transportation.

Problems identified in cases can be classified into: *problems of technical failures* (for example, in case 1 there were delays due to LexNET overload); *problems of unavailability of participants* (for example, in case 4, the lawyer demanded an in-person meeting, not trusting video communication); *problems of legal conflicts* (in particular, in case 3 it was necessary to quickly adapt the procedural rules for blockchain).[99]

Spain is actively introducing European digital standards into its judicial system. The key documents are:

The eIDAS Regulation (910/2014) is the basis for electronic identification. All court documents are signed by a qualified electronic signature (QES). In 2022, for example, 2.3 million documents with an eIDAS signature were submitted through LexNET. Civil servants use professional eIDAS certificates, and citizens use national electronic IDs (DNIe). Integration with Cl @ ve platform (government authentication system). Support for European trust nodes (eIDAS Network).

Directive (EU) 2016/680 - data protection in justice (automated pseudonyms of cases, strict requirements for the storage of electronic evidence). Example: In 2021, the Supreme Court reversed the decision due to violations in the digital processing of personal data.

The e-Justice initiative is the creation of a pan-European digital legal space. The European portal e-Justice provides Spanish courts with access to the precedents of the ECHR, and also implements a mechanism for multilingual translation of documents. Spain participates in pilot projects on electronic: delivery of court documents, obtaining evidence from other EU countries. It is important to note that the unresolved problems of implementing EU legislation into the Spanish legal system are: technical problems (incompatibility of some national systems with European standards. Example: until 2020, LexNET did not support all eIDAS formats) and legal problems (conflicts between the GDPR and the national data protection law, difficulties in recognizing foreign eIDs in criminal proceedings.

The new EU requirements (in 2023-2024) were: the mandatory use of the European digital wallet (EU Digital Identity Wallet), the expansion of eIDAS for

---

[99] Grudtsyna L.Y. Digital Justice in Spain//Digital Law. 2024. № 4. S. 46-48.

decentralized identifiers, the introduction of AI Act into judicial analytical systems (see Table 1).

Table 1. Statistics on the introduction of digitalization in Spanish legal proceedings.

Indicator	2021	2023
Documents with eIDAS signature	1.8 million	3.2 million
Vessels connected to e-CODEX	23%	68%
Cross-border electronic interaction cases	542	1,890

Let's consider several cases of application of eIDAS in the judicial practice of Spain.

Case number 1. Appeal to the Supreme Court (2022). Case: *Bankia vs. Grupo Inmobiliario* (€4.7 million commercial dispute). Application of eIDAS: all documents were submitted through the LexNET system with qualified electronic signatures (QES). The foreign witness testified via eIDAS identification (using Estonian digital ID). Result: The review period was reduced from 18 to 6 months. First recognition of cross-border eIDAS authentication in a Spanish commercial process.

Case number 2. Criminal case (Audiensia Nacional, 2021). Case: Investigation of cyber fraud using fake certificates. Application of eIDAS: the court requested QES verification through the Spanish trust node (TS @). 147 electronic documents were authenticated in 3 days (the usual examination took 2-3 weeks). Precedent: recognition of electronic evidence with an eIDAS signature as equivalent to paper.

Case number 3. Labour dispute (Court of Barcelona, 2023). Case: a remote worker disputed the dismissal. Application of eIDAS: the contract and notice of dismissal are signed by mobile QES (used by DNIe 3.0). The video session was conducted with eIDAS identification of the parties. As a result, a precedent of remote labor justice was created. Compensation paid through electronic court payment.

Case number 4. Family Law (Court of Valencia, 2022). Case: Division of property involving a German citizen. Application of eIDAS: the German side submitted documents through EU Login. Notarial acts are certified by the European seal of trust. Feature: the first use of eIDAS notarization in Spanish family law.

At the same time, there are so-called "problem cases," which include the following:

Case number 1: Verification error (Malaga Court, 2021). Rejection of the claim due to incorrect QES-certificate of the French company. Problem: Trust registries are out of sync.

Case number 2: eIDAS restrictions (National Court, 2020). Refusal to allow cryptographic signatures (not corresponding to eIDAS). Consequence: tougher checks on digital evidence. eIDAS has become the standard for: electronic document management, cross-border cases, expedited procedures. Currently, there is a pilot project on eIDAS 2.0 in the Supreme Court (2024), integration with the European Blockchain Service (EBSI).

The main directions of digitalization of legal proceedings in Spain:

1. Electronic justice (Justicia Digital). Since 2016, the Justicia Digital platform has been operating in Spain, providing: filing lawsuits and petitions in electronic form, notifying the parties through a single portal, and accessing court decisions in digital format.

2. Virtual court hearings. The COVID-19 pandemic accelerated the introduction of videoconferencing in litigation. Spanish courts use LexNET and Poder Judicial Virtual platforms for remote meetings.

3. Artificial intelligence and automation. Pilot projects using AI include: analysis of judicial practice to predict decisions, automatic processing of routine requests (for example, debt collection).

Despite progress, the following challenges remain to be addressed in the coming years:

A. Digital inequality - not all citizens have access to technology.

B. Cybersecurity - risks of data leaks and cyberattacks.

B. Legal conflicts - the need to harmonize digital solutions with traditional procedural rules.

Thus, Spain has shown significant success in digitalizing justice, but further improvement in infrastructure and legal regulation is required to fully integrate technology. [100]The experience of the Spanish system can be useful for other countries implementing e-justice. Results achieved (for 2023): [101]more than 90% of vessels are connected to LexNET 2.0; reduction of case processing time by 15-20% due to automation; increase in the number of electronic claims to 70% of the total. The next stage of digitalization (2025-2026) may include: a complete transition to "cloud justice" (using cloud technologies for storing data), the development of a blockchain for verifying court decisions, and even greater introduction of AI (for example, chat bots for consultations). [102]Thus, the 2019-2023 Plan was an important step in the digital transformation of Spanish justice. Although not all goals have been fully achieved, Spain has entered the top 5 EU countries in terms of the level of digitalization of the judicial system. Further development will require investment in infrastructure and training for judges, lawyers and citizens.[103]

Spain demonstrates, firstly, the successful integration of eIDAS into national systems, and secondly, active participation in pan-European digital projects. At the same time, in our opinion, the need for further harmonization of legislation is

[100]European Commission. (2020). Digitalisation of justice in the EU.
[101]Report on the implementation of the plan (2023): Ministry of Justice Spain.
Official CGPJ [102]website:.https://www.poderjudicial.es
[103]Grudtsyna L.Y. Digitalization of justice in the European Union//International Scientific Bulletin. 2025. № 7. S. 198-204.

important. Prospects are: full transition to EU Digital Identity Wallet by 2026 and participation in testing blockchain solutions for cross-border justice.

3.4. E-JUSTICE IN LATVIA AND LITHUANIA

Latvia is actively developing digital tools in the judicial system, striving for a complete digital transformation by 2025. Although the process is slower than in Slovenia, the country has already implemented several key solutions. The legislative basis for these decisions was:

Electronic Document Management Act (2002, as amended in 2021). Equates electronic documents with a qualified electronic signature (CEP) to paper.

The Court Digitalization Plan (2021-2025), which obliged all courts to switch to electronic records management and integrate with the e-Courts system, established standards for electronic filing and video conferencing (VCC).

The main platforms and services in Latvia are:

- "e-Courts" system (e-Tiesas), the [104] functionality of which includes: filing claims, complaints and petitions, access to case materials for participants in the process, notification of meetings and decisions. It is important to note that at present (2025) filing of claims, complaints and petitions to Latvian courts is still available only for civil and administrative cases, and criminal cases are conducted in a hybrid format (partially paper).[105]

The legislative basis for the functioning of the e-Tiesas system in Latvia is:

---

[104]Official website:https://manas.tiesas.lv

[105]Grudtsyna L.Y. Issues of the organization of electronic justice in the European Union//Research Institute for Education and Law. 2025. № 1-3. S. 14-18.

- *The Latvian Judicial Power Act* 1992 (*Latvijas Republikas tiesu varas likums*), which established the right of courts to use electronic document management and established the mandatory electronic publication of decisions (except in closed cases). The Latvian Judicial Power Law is the main regulatory act regulating the organization and activities of the Latvian judicial system. The law consists of 15 sections, the key of which are presented in Table 1.

Table 1. Main sections of the Latvian Law "On Judicial Power" of 1992

Section	**Contents**	**Practical significance**
I. General provisions	Defines the **principles of the judiciary**: independence, legality, publicity.	Guarantees the independence of judges from the executive.
II. Judicial system	It lists the **types of courts:** • Constitutional Court , • Supreme Court , • District and District Courts.	Delimits jurisdiction (e.g., criminal cases begin in district courts).
III. Status of judges	Requirements for judges (citizenship, education, seniority), procedure for appointment and removal.	Judges of the Supreme Court are appointed by the Seimas for life (art. 52).
IV. Organization of the work of courts	Rules for the formation of judicial compositions, distribution of cases.	Automatic distribution of cases through **e-Tiesas** to eliminate corruption.
V. Judicial proceedings	Principles of the process: adversarial, language of proceedings (Latvian), right to defense.	Criminal cases can be considered in Russian if the accused does not speak Latvian.
VI. Financing of ships	The budget of the courts is formed separately from other branches of government.	Courts are not dependent on the Ministry of Justice for funding.
X. E-Justice (added in 2020)	Fixes the use of **e-Tiesas**, electronic signature, video conferencing.	Basis for digitalization (e.g. online filing).

Key legal rules and their application:

Independence of judges (art. 5). Judges cannot be dismissed for making "inconvenient" decisions. In 2023, the Latvian Constitutional Court overturned the Sejm's attempt to remove a judge for criticizing the government.

Language of proceedings (art. 18). In 2024, the Riga District Court allowed a hearing in Russian in a fraud case (the accused is a non-citizen of Latvia).

Electronic justice (art. 45.1). Through **e-Tiesas**, 72% of civil lawsuits were filed in 2023 (Justice Department data).

Openness of decisions (Art. 24). All decisions (except for state secrets) are published on the **Latvija.lv**. In 2022, the Supreme Court of Latvia ordered the courts to anonymize the names of the participants in the cases.

In 2024, a package of important amendments was adopted to the 1992 Latvian Law on the Judiciary, including: an amendment to Art. 45.1, according to which since 2025 all Latvian courts are obliged to accept documents only through e-Tiesas (exception - criminal cases). The need for these changes caused an increase in the budget of Latvian vessels by 10% in 2025 to modernize the IT infrastructure. The Law "On the Judiciary" ensures the stability of the judicial system, but requires improvements: Latvia should adopt the Estonian experience of speeding up processes and the Lithuanian approach to integrating criminal proceedings into the digital environment.[106]

Cabinet Regulation No. 400 (2022) approved technical standards for e-Tiesas: file formats (PDF/A, XML), qualified electronic signature (CEP) requirements, and also required courts to accept documents electronically from 2023.

Table 2. Comparison of digitalization of justice in Latvia with Estonia and Lithuania.

---

[106]Grudtsyna L.Y. Digitalization of justice in the European Union//International Scientific Bulletin. 2025. № 7. S. 198-204.

Criterion	Latvia	Estonia	Lithuania
Appointment of judges	Sejm (Parliament)	President	Special Commission under the President
E-Justice	e-Tiesas (c 2019)	e-toimik (c 2005)	e.teismas.lt (c 2018)
Timing of cases	8 months (civil)	4 months.	6 months.

The National Plan for the Digitalization of Justice of Latvia (2021-2027) is a strategic roadmap aimed at a complete transition to e-justice by 2027. The plan is funded from the EU budget (€23 million) and national sources (€7 million).

Table 3. Tasks of digitalization of justice in Latvia.

Priority	Tasks	Terms
1. Full integration of e-Tiesas	Connection of all courts, including criminal and administrative	2025-2026
2. Process Automation	Implement AI to analyze claims, predict solutions	2024 (pilot)
3. Cyberimmunity	Data protection (ISO 27001), backup data centers	2023-2025
4. Access for citizens	Mobile application, multilingual interface (Latvian, Russian)	2026
5. Interstate Integration	Connecting to EU e-Justice Portal for cross-border cases	2024

Plans for the development of Latvian legal proceedings for 2024-2027. involves the expansion of the functionality of e-Tiesas involves in 2025 - the launch of a module for criminal cases (pilot in the Riga District Court), in 2026 - an AI assistant for judges (analysis of precedents, verification of deadlines). By 2026, it is planned to switch to blockchain for document verification, as well as add Russian and English to the interface. The strengths of digitalization in Latvia are: good integration of e-Tiesas, EU support, focus on cybersecurity. How e-Tiesas works on the official portal https://manas.tiesas.lvis shown in the table below.

Table 4. Main functions of the e-Tiesas portal.

Functionality	Description	Case Study
1. Submission of documents	Claims, complaints, petitions are uploaded through your personal account.	The lawyer files a lawsuit to recover the debt without attending court.
2. Electronic case (e-lieta)	All materials are stored digitally, available to the judge and parties.	The judge checks the evidence online without requiring paper copies.
3. Notices	The system sends SMS/email notifications about meetings and decisions.	Plaintiff receives 14 days notice of hearing date.
4. Video conferencing (VC)	Meetings are held through TET Video Conference (state standard of Latvia).	A witness from Germany testifies remotely.
5. Public Access	Impersonal decisions are published on the Latvija.lv.	The journalist studies statistics on labor disputes.

In Latvia, since 2011, a digital gateway to public services and justice has been operating - the state portal "Latvija.lv," [107]which provides access to public information: court decisions (anonymized), the register of enforcement proceedings and data on judges and courts. **In the Register of enforcement proceedings ("Ippildītāju reš istrs") you can check: the presence of debts from individuals/legal entities, the status of enforcement proceedings. Currently, the official language** of the state portal "Latvija.lv" is Latvian, but by 2026 it is planned to introduce multilingualism (adding Russian and English). In addition, by 2026, AI search by the judicial practice data bank and blockchain verification will be introduced.[108]

[107]Official address:https://www.latvija.lv

[108]Grudtsyna L.Y. Digitalization of justice in Latvia and Lithuania: theoretical and legal review//Humanities. High School. 2025. № 1. S. 59-64.

Latvia is ahead of Romania, but lags behind Slovenia in the digitalization of justice. The main problems are technical risks and conservatism of judges. However, by 2025, the country may reach the level of CEE leaders (like Estonia).

Lithuania is one of the leaders in the Baltic region in digitalizing the judicial system, introducing modern technologies to increase the transparency, accessibility and efficiency of justice. Lithuania's legal framework in the field of digital justice is considered one of the most progressive in the Baltic States. The key act is the Law on Electronic Justice (No. XIII-1424), adopted in 2018 and updated in 2023. Its main goal is to ensure a complete transition to electronic document management in courts by 2026.

The main provisions of the Electronic Justice Act (No. XIII-1424) regulate:

1. Electronic document management (Articles 5-9). All procedural documents are submitted only in electronic form through the e.teismas.lt system (the exception is criminal cases with material evidence). Electronic documents with a qualified signature (CEP) are equated to paper.

2. Electronic case (e-byla) (arts. 10-12). All case materials are stored in a single digital system available to judges and trial parties. Automatic notification of participants about new documents.

3. Videoconferencing (Art. 15). Courts are required to hold meetings through MS Teams or Zoom at the request of the parties.

4. Data openness (art. 18). Impersonal decisions are published on e.teismai.lv within 3 days of issuance.

5. Sanctions for non-performance (art. 22). The judge's refusal to accept electronic documents entails disciplinary responsibility.

The Lithuanian law on electronic justice is one of the most advanced in the European Union, but requires: firstly, expansion into criminal cases, secondly, improving the Internet infrastructure in the regions, and thirdly, further integration with EU e-Justice. If these trends continue, then by 2026 Lithuania will catch up with Estonia in terms of digitalization.

In addition to the Law on Electronic Justice (No. XIII-1424), Lithuania has: The National Digital Transformation Strategy (2021-2030), which includes the full transition of ships to electronic document management by 2025, and amendments to the Lithuanian CPC and Lithuanian CPC (2022)

The main platform of the electronic court in Lithuania is the portal "e.teismas.lt" (Electronic Court). [109]The functionality of the portal includes filing claims, appeals, petitions; conducting an electronic file (e-byla), in which all materials are stored in digital format; notification of meetings and decisions through the personal account. The portal mainly works for civil, administrative and economic cases, and criminal cases are conducted in electronic form - partially (currently the stage of introduction of an electronic court in criminal cases).

Lithuania is demonstrating a rapid pace of digitalization and could become a model for other European Union countries in the coming years. The e.teismai.lt system provides a convenient and transparent mechanism for monitoring enforcement proceedings. Although the service requires some improvements, it greatly simplifies the interaction of citizens with the Lithuanian judicial system.

3.5. ELECTRONIC JUSTICE IN ESTONIA

Estonia is currently a world leader in the digital transformation of public services, including the judicial system. Since the 2000s the country has been actively introducing

[109]Official website:https://e.teismas.lt

electronic solutions into justice, which over 25 years has significantly increased the efficiency, transparency and accessibility of trials. The principles of digital justice in Estonia are: the principle of electronic identification (e-ID, Mobiil-ID), the principle of complete digitalization of document circulation and the principle of data openness (public registers of court decisions).

The Estonian e-justice system is based on the following legal acts:

- The Estonian Digital Signature Act (2000), legalized the use of electronic signatures in legal proceedings.
- The Estonian Electronic Data Interchange Act (2004) provided the legal basis for electronic document management.
- Amendments to the Estonian Civil Procedure Code and the Estonian Code of Criminal Procedure (2008-2020), allowed online filing of lawsuits, holding meetings via video link and using electronic evidence.

Let's take a closer look at these regulations.

The adoption ***of the Digital*** *Signatures Act* (*2000*) in Estonia was a key step in creating the infrastructure *of the* electronic state. This law not only legalized the use of electronic signatures, but also laid the foundation for digital litigation in Estonia, making it more efficient, transparent and accessible. The law established a legal framework for the use of electronic signatures, equating them with handwritten ones in cases where: the signature meets the requirements of a qualified electronic signature (CEP); certified signing tool (e-ID, Mobiil-ID, Smart-ID) is used.

The main principles established by this Law are: a) technological neutrality - various methods of creating a signature are allowed if they provide the necessary level of security; b) recognition of foreign certificates in accordance with Estonian standards; c) responsibility of certification centers for reliability of issued certificates. Since 2002, electronic signatures have been used in Estonian legal proceedings, which allowed: firstly, to file claims and petitions online; secondly, to sign protocols and court decisions in digital format; thirdly, to hold remote meetings with legally significant authentication of participants. Electronic signatures are used in: e-File - electronic document management system; e-Court, a platform for remote meetings; X-Road - a secure environment for data exchange between ships and government agencies.[110]

In Estonia, there are three options for electronic user identification: e-ID (electronic ID-card), Mobiil-ID (signing documents via SIM-card), Smart-ID (mobile application for authentication). In civil and arbitration cases, it is possible to file claims and sign settlement agreements electronically, as well as remote (online) court hearings (e-Court) using secure data exchange (encryption, blockchain), in criminal cases electronic interrogation protocols (e-File) are used.

The advantages of electronic justice are a reduction in the time for consideration of cases (by 30-40%), a reduction in the cost of paper document circulation, as well as an increase in transparency (all documents are stored in a digital archive). Along with the advantages, there are problems associated with the digitalization of justice, and the most serious of them are cybersecurity problems (in particular, the risks of hacking e-ID, as it was in 2017), legal conflicts (for example, recognition of Estonian electronic signatures abroad) and the problem of access (Internet coverage about 92%) and increasing citizens' confidence in electronic justice (the need to train the population in digital literacy).

It is also interesting to note the fact that the experience of Estonia is borrowed by the countries of the European Union, in particular, on the basis of Estonian legislation, the European Union Regulation eIDAS was developed and adopted on July 23, 2014, which regulates the use of electronic identification and trust services for electronic transactions within the EU. The reliable technological infrastructure developed in Estonia, coupled with a systematic approach to digitalization and the use of blockchain

[110]Grudtsyna L.Y. Digital Justice in Estonia//Digital Law. 2024. № 4. S. 59-65.

systems, have made Estonian electronic justice one of the world's examples at the moment.

The adoption ***of the Electronic*** *Data Exchange Act* (2004) was an important step in the development *of* Estonia's digital infrastructure. This law became the foundation of the digital state of Estonia and created legal conditions for the safe and effective exchange of electronic documents between government agencies, business and citizens, laying the foundation for full-fledged electronic document management. The law established the following basic norms:

Recognition of the legal force of electronic documents - equated them to paper ones, subject to the requirements for authenticity and integrity.

Requirements for data formats - approved information structuring standards (XML, JSON).

Electronic signature regulation - mandatory use of qualified signatures (e-ID, Mobiil-ID) for legally significant transactions.

The principle of one-time provision of data is a ban on duplicate requests for information from citizens.

To implement the law, the X-Road platform was developed - a secure system for interdepartmental data exchange, and data registration centers were created - unified registers (population, enterprises, real estate). A serious economic effect of the use of blockchain technologies and a decrease in paper workflow, as well as the use of AI in legal proceedings in Estonia, was a reduction in administrative expenses by 2% of GDP annually. However, it is important to understand that the success of the Electronic Data Interchange Act in Estonia was made possible primarily due to the innovative IT infrastructure in the country (without it, not a single legislative framework, no matter how progressive it may be, could put into practice blockchain technologies and the use of AI in processing procedural documents), an advanced legislative framework and a systematic approach to the implementation of the tasks.

Estonia in the period 2008-2020. carried out a large-scale reform of procedural legislation. ***The amendments to the Estonian Code of Civil Procedure and the Estonian Code of Criminal Procedure*** were aimed at digitalizing the judicial system and contain three key innovations: filing claims in electronic form, conducting court hearings via video link and using electronic evidence. Particular attention is paid to the technological and legal aspects of implementing these changes, as well as their impact on the effectiveness of justice.

The 2010 amendments introduced Article 244^{1} in the Estonian Civil Procedure Code, which establishes: a) equal legal force of electronic and paper claims, b) mandatory use of a qualified electronic signature, c) requirements for electronic document formats. At the same time, the technical implementation of these amendments is important (and the IT infrastructure was prepared in advance), which by the time of their adoption could provide round-the-clock submission of documents, automated verification of formal requirements and integration with state registers. As a result (over 10 years, by 2020), 94% of civil claims are filed electronically, processing time has been reduced from 5 to 1 working day, and the number of technical failures was less than 0.5% of cases. Amendments to the Estonian Code of Criminal Procedure (Article 231^{5}) and the Estonian Code of Civil Procedure (Article 155^{3}) enshrined: the right of the court to conduct court hearings remotely; list of cases of mandatory use of HQS; technical requirements for equipment and its safety.

The e-Court system allows: to ensure the participation of parties from anywhere in the world, to record and archive meetings, to use an automated protocol. Important, currently unresolved problems are: identification of participants (solution - e-ID), technical failures (solution can be backup communication channels), as well as ensuring confidentiality (strengthening encryption).

Amendments to the Estonian Civil Procedure Code in 2016 introduced: the concept of "electronic evidence" (Article 112^{4}), admissibility criteria (integrity, authenticity) and rules for research in court. As reliability technologies are used:

blockchain storage (KSI Blockchain), hash sums for verification and digital timestamps. Thus, the 2008-2020 amendments to Estonian civil and criminal procedural legislation have created one of the most advanced e-justice models in the world. Further development involves: the introduction of artificial intelligence for preliminary assessment of cases, the expansion of interstate electronic interaction, as well as the improvement of cyber defense systems.

The Estonian technology platform X-Road should be mentioned separately as ***the basis for secure interdepartmental*** electronic interaction in the Estonian judicial system, providing secure data exchange between judicial authorities and other Estonian state institutions. The X-Road system was developed in 2001 and introduced into the Estonian judicial system in 2008. In the context of judicial activity, X-Road ensures the integration of courts with 15 key state registers of Estonia, which radically changed the judicial processes and significantly increased its efficiency. [111]The basic principles of building this system are: decentralized architecture, the principle of minimum necessary access, end-to-end data encryption, as well as the principle of using blockchain technology to ensure the invariability of access logs. The components of the system are: Central Server, Security Servers, Certification Center (CA) and Center of Registers.[112]

The functionality of X-Road in the judicial system allows integration with such state registers as: population register, land cadastre, vehicle register and register of entrepreneurs. Automated services for judges are: a service for verifying the identity of participants in the process, a service for requesting information about real estate, a service for obtaining data on criminal convictions and a service for verifying the registration data of legal entities.

The adoption *of the Personal Data Protection Ordinance (Isikuandmete kaitse seadus)* in 2008 was an important step in the development of Estonian legislation aimed

[111]Estonian Information System Authority. X-Road Technical Specifications. 2020.
[112]Grudtsyna L.Y. Digitalization of justice in the European Union//International Scientific Bulletin. 2025. № 7. S. 198-204.

at regulating the processing of personal data in the face of the rapid digitalization of public services. [113] This regulation not only ensured the implementation of EU directives, but also created a unique model of privacy protection compatible with the principles of the "electronic state." The Estonian Personal Data Protection [114]Ordinance (2008) regulates the processing of personal data by both public and private organizations, applies to automated and non-automated processing systems, and also establishes special rules for sensitive data (biometric, genetic, medical). This Decree established the principleof "once-only" (single data submission), logging of all requests for personal data, and also established the rules for using the blockchain (KSI) to control integrity.[115]

Estonian regulation 2008 became the basis for early implementation of GDPR (*General Data Protection Regulation*) - the general data protection regulation, the main EU law on the protection of personal data, which entered into force on May 25, 2018. Subsequently, [116]GDPR became a model for similar laws in other countries (for example, LGPD in Brazil, CCPA in California), strengthened the protection of user privacy on the Internet and forced companies to revise data collection policies. [117]In general, the X-Road system has proven its effectiveness as the technological basis for the digital transformation of the Estonian judicial system. The unique combination of safety, reliability and convenience has made it a model for creating similar systems in other countries. The further development of the platform opens up new prospects for a fully digital justice ecosystem.

The e-File system, introduced in Estonian judicial practice in 2005, is a comprehensive solution for electronic court proceedings, covering all stages of the trial - from filing a statement of claim to the execution of a court decision.

---

[113]Krull L. Secure Data Exchange in E-Government. Springer, 2018.
[114]European Commission. e-Justice Report. 2021.
[115]Grudtsyna L.Y. Digitalization of justice in Latvia and Lithuania: theoretical and legal review//Humanities. High School. 2025. № 1. S. 59-64.
[116]The GDPR replaced the 95/46/EC Directive and established uniform strict rules for the processing of personal data within the European Union.
[117]OECD. Digital Government in Estonia. 2019.

Table 1.

№	*E-File Functionality*	
1.	For process participants	• Electronic filing of procedural documents • Case Progress Notices • Remote familiarization with case materials • Electronic payment of court expenses
2.	For judges and court staff	• Automated distribution of cases • Electronic signing of judicial acts • Statistical reporting • Tools for teamwork
3.	For authorities	• Monitoring the judicial burden • Analysis of judicial statistics • Resource Planning

The system has become an important component of the digital ecosystem of Estonian justice, providing a full cycle of electronic document management. The e-File system is a single repository of court cases, with an integrated electronic filing system, an automated document management module and an integration gateway with other government systems and platforms.[118]

Table 2.

№	**Impact *of* e-File on judicial efficiency**	
1.	Operational Benefits	• 40% reduction in case processing time • Reduce procedural errors • Reduced document processing effort
2.	Economic effect	• Reduce paper costs • Optimization of staffing • Reduce archive storage costs

[118]Tamm M. "e-Justice in Estonia". Springer, 2021.

3.	Social benefits	• Improving access to justice • Convenience for process participants • Transparency of judicial activities

Thus, the e-File system in Estonia has become an important element of the digital transformation of the Estonian judicial system, ensuring a high level of efficiency, transparency and accessibility of justice. The experience of its implementation and operation is of significant interest to other countries engaged in the digitalization of judicial systems.[119]

The e-Court system, officially introduced in Estonia in 2019, is a technological platform for holding a full cycle of court hearings in a remote format. Developed as a logical continuation of the digital transformation of the Estonian judicial system, it provides up to 95% of procedural actions without the physical presence of participants. The basic components of this system are: a video conferencing module (based on WebRTC), a court session management system, an integrated logging complex and a participant verification module. The e-Court system is integrated with the e-File system and has access to public registers via X-Road.

The main functions of the e-Court system are: video communication with multi-channel audio, collaboration with documents, electronic signing of protocols and automatic transcription of speech (for example, electronic court records). Important and already indispensable tools of work were: a virtual queue of speeches, private consulting rooms, an emergency communication system with technical support and a language translation module (Estonian-Russian). As of 2023, 89% [120]of civil cases, 76% of criminal proceedings involving defenders and all administrative proceedings were remotely examined in Estonian courts.[121]

[119]eIDAS Regulation (EU) No 910/2014.
[120]European Commission. "Digitalisation of Justice" (2022).
[121]Estonian Judiciary Annual Report 2023.

The European portal ***e-Justice***, created to digitalize legal services in the EU, actively integrates technological and legal solutions developed by Estonia. The European e-Justice Portal () https://e-justice.europa.euis a single digital platform that provides access to legal services in EU countries. Estonia, as a leader in the field of the digital state, has become a key supplier of technological solutions for this project. The main borrowings from the Estonian model were: electronic identification, interdepartmental data exchange, electronic legal proceedings and blockchain for data protection. Let's consider them in more detail in Table 3.

Table 3.

	Implementation of the Estonian e-justice model by the European Union		
.	**Electronic identification (eIDAS and Estonian e-ID)**	The Estonian e-ID system (based on ID cards and Mobiil-ID) formed the basis of the European regulation eIDAS (2014), which unified the electronic signature in the EU.	EU citizens can log in to the e-Justice Portal through national e-IDs, as in Estonia. Notarial documents signed by e-IDs are recognized in all EU countries.
.	**Inter-agency data exchange (similar to X-Road)**	The Estonian X-Road technology (decentralized data exchange) inspired the creation of the European Interoperability Framework (EIF).	The e-Justice Portal has implemented a mechanism for requesting national registers (e.g. criminal record checks) similar to the Estonian integration of ships with registers via X-Road.
.	**E-Court (e-File and e-Court)**	The Estonian e-File and e-Court systems became prototypes for the e-Justice modules.	In the European portal, you can file claims in some EU courts online (as in e-File). EU video session pilots use the Estonian e-Court experience.
.	**Blockchain for Data Protection (KSI Blockchain)**	Estonia was the first to implement blockchain (Keyless Signature	The e-Justice Portal uses a European trusted time stamp

		Infrastructure, KSI) to protect legal documents.	system (similar to KSI) to verify documents.

Estonia has proved that the complete digitalization of justice is possible. Her experience shows that the key to success lies in a strong legislative framework, innovative technologies and openness of the judicial system. Development [122]prospects include increased use of AI and international standardization of digital justice.[123]

Table 4.

№	Estonian technologies and their analogues in the EU	
	Technology (Estonia)	Analogue in e-Justice Portal (EU)
1.	e-ID / Mobiil-ID	eIDAS-compliant identification
2.	X-Road	European Interoperability Framework (EIF)
3.	e-File	European Claims System
4.	e-Court	Video Session Pilots
5.	KSI Blockchain	EU Trusted Timestamping

Thus, it can be concluded that Estonian developments have become the basis for the key functions of the e-Justice Portal, including: unified electronic identification (eIDAS), secure data exchange (analogues of X-Road), electronic legal proceedings (e-File/e-Court), document protection technologies (blockchain).

3.6. E-JUSTICE IN ROMANIA AND SLOVENIA

The digitalization of the judicial system is one of the priorities of the modern rule of law. Romania, as a member of the European Union, is actively introducing electronic services into its judicial system, following pan-European trends. One of the key elements of this transformation is the electronic filing of claims. The electronic filing of claims in Romania is regulated by Law No. 135/2010 on the Code of Civil

[122]e-Estonia. How Estonia's X-Road Powers Digital Government. 2022.
[123]E-Estonia. (2023). Digital Court System.

Procedure, which provides for the use of electronic means in judicial proceedings. In addition, the National Digital Agenda Strategy for Romania (*Strategia Naí ionalí privind Agenda Digitalí pentru România*) promotes the development of electronic services in the judicial system. [124]Since the introduction of electronic filing of claims through the Electronic Justice Portal (*Portalul Justişiei Electronice*), there has been a steady increase in the use of this service. Below are the statistics for five years (2018-2022):

Year	Number of electronic claims	Share of total number of claims (%)
2018	15,000	10%
2019	30,000	20%
2020	60,000	40%
2021	90,000	60%
2022	120,000	75%

The electronic filing of claims has a significant impact on the Romanian judicial system given the following positive effects:

1. Reduce case processing time. The automation of the process of filing claims in Romania reduces the time for processing documents and speeds up the start of the trial. According to the Romanian Ministry of Justice, the average time for handling cases has decreased by 30% since the introduction of electronic filing.[125]

2. Increased availability of justice. Electronic filing in Romania makes justice more accessible to citizens, especially those living in remote areas. This reduces the need for personal visits to courts and reduces the cost of participating in trials.

3. Reduction of administrative burden. The use of electronic services reduces the administrative burden on Romanian courts and their staff, allowing them to focus on cases.

[124]Portalul Justiției Electronice. [Electronic Resource]. URL: https://portal.just.ro.

[125]Grudtsyna L.Y. Digitalization of justice in Romania and Slovenia: theoretical and legal review//Humanities. High School. 2025. № 1. S. 28-35.

This paragraph examines the 10 most important areas of digitalization of the judicial system and proceedings in Romania, the application of which demonstrates the effectiveness of the use of electronic means in litigation in Romania: (1) electronic filing of a claim; (2) holding a court session via videoconferencing; (3) electronic notification of the hearing; (4) online payment of court fees; (5) publication of the judgment on the ReJust portal; (6) use of electronic signature; (7) search for court decisions through Portal Jurisprudenthe; (8) electronic access to legislation through Portal Legislativ; (9) online mediation; (10) the use of artificial intelligence to analyze court decisions. Let's look at them in more detail.

1. Electronic filing of a claim. The introduction of an electronic filing system in Romania was made possible by a number of legislative changes aimed at digitalizing justice. [126]The main regulations governing this process are:

- *Electronic Signature Act (Act No.* 455/2001). This Act established the legal basis for the use of electronic documents and signatures in the judicial system.
- *The Law on Judicial Reform (2018).* This law provided for the introduction of electronic filing of claims as part of a comprehensive reform aimed at modernizing the judicial system.
- *Romanian Code of Civil Procedure.* In 2020, the code was amended to allow electronic filing of claims.

These regulations have created a legal framework for the use of electronic filing of claims, ensuring their validity and recognition in judicial practice. [127] The introduction of an electronic filing system required the creation of a technical infrastructure that would ensure reliable and secure data transmission. In Romania, the National Electronic Filing System (SNEPI) was developed for this purpose, which includes three elements: a) an electronic platform (each court in Romania has access to a centralized platform through which claims can be filed), b) integration with judicial

[126]Strategia Națională privind Agenda Digitală pentru România (2014).
[127]European Commission. Report on the digitalization of justice in EU countries (2022).

systems (the platform is integrated with the main judicial systems, which allows automatic loading of claims and attached documents), c) an electronic signature (claims are signed by an electronic signature of the plaintiff or his representative, which ensures their authenticity). [128]It is important to note that this system provides fast and reliable data transfer, reducing the time and cost of their processing.[129]

2. Conducting a court session via videoconferencing (VCC). The use of videoconferencing in judicial proceedings is regulated by Law No. 135/2010 on the Romanian Code of Civil Procedure, as well as by a number of bylaws adopted within the framework of the National Digital Agenda Strategy (Strategia Na¶ ionalí privind Agenda Digitalpentí ru România). These documents provide for the possibility of holding meetings online, especially in cases where the physical presence of the parties is difficult. Since the introduction of HQS technology into the Romanian judicial system, there has been a steady increase in its use. [130]The use of HQS has a significant impact on the Romanian judicial system:

- *Reduction of case processing time.* Meetings held through the CCS can reduce the time required to organize processes, especially when participants are located in different geographical locations. According to the Romanian Ministry of Justice, the average time for handling cases has decreased by 25% since the introduction of the HQS;
- *Making justice more accessible.* HQS makes justice more accessible to citizens, especially those who live in remote areas or cannot physically attend court for valid reasons (for example, due to health conditions);
- *resource savings.* The use of HQS reduces the cost of transport and the organization of meetings, which is especially important for participants in processes and the judicial system as a whole.

---

[128]Legea nr. 135/2010 privind Codul de procedură civilă.

[129]Report of the Romanian Ministry of Justice on the implementation of electronic filing of claims (2021).

[130]Grudtsyna L.Y. Digitalization of justice and use of electronic means in litigation in Romania//Digital law. 2025. № 1. S. 48-55.

For further successful use of videoconferencing, it is necessary to: a) improve technical infrastructure, especially in rural and remote areas; b) train judges, lawyers and citizens to work with HQS technology; c) strengthen cybersecurity measures to protect confidential information; d) develop a clear legal framework for the use of HQS in various types of litigation. [131]However, to fully realize the potential of the CCS, it is necessary to overcome the existing challenges associated with technical limitations, digital literacy and security issues. Successful implementation of these tasks will enable Romania to create a modern and effective judicial system that meets the standards of the European Union.[132]

3. Electronic notice of court hearing. The introduction of electronic notice of court hearings in Romania was made possible by a number of legislative changes aimed at digitalizing the judicial system. The main regulations governing this process are: ***The Law on Electronic Signature*** **(Law No. 455/2001)*, the Law on Judicial Reform*** (Law No. 304/2018) **and *the Romanian Code of Civil Procedure***. In 2020, the Code was amended to allow the use of electronic notifications in civil proceedings. These regulations have created a legal basis for the use of electronic notifications, ensuring their validity and recognition in judicial practice. It should also be noted that the introduction of electronic notification required the creation of a technical infrastructure that would ensure reliable and secure transmission of notifications. In Romania, the **National Electronic Notification System (SINE) has been developed for this purpose,** which includes the following elements: (1) **court e-mail** (each court has received an official e-mail address through which notifications are sent), (2) **an electronic signature** (notifications are signed by an electronic signature of a judge or court clerk, which ensures their authenticity), (3) **a notification platform** (a centralized platform that allows participants in the process to receive notifications through a personal account).[133]

[131]Legea nr. 135/2010 privind Codul de procedură civilă.
[132]Popescu, A. (2021). Digital Transformation of the Judiciary in Romania: Challenges and Opportunities. Journal of Legal Studies, 15(2), 45-60.
[133]Report of the Romanian Ministry of Justice on the implementation of the electronic notification (2021).

The introduction of electronic notification of court hearings in Romania has also led to a number of positive results, which include, inter alia, increasing the accessibility and transparency of justice for citizens, improving the quality of protection of violated rights and freedoms of citizens, reducing costs and reducing the time for consideration of court cases. However, the introduction of electronic notification has also faced a number of challenges, including low levels of digital literacy among some stakeholders and technical failures in the system.

4. Online payment of court fees. The introduction of online payment of court fees in Romania was made possible by a number of legislative changes aimed at digitalizing the judicial system. The main regulations governing this process are also***:*** ***The Law on Electronic Signature*** **(Law No. 455/2001), the** ***Law on Judicial Reform*** *(*Law No. 304/2018) and ***the Romanian Code of Civil Procedure.*** [134]In 2020, the Code was amended to allow the use of online payments to pay court fees. The introduction of online payment of court fees in Romania is an important step in the digitalization of justice. This innovation contributes to improving the efficiency of the judicial system, the availability of justice and reducing costs.

5. The publication of the judgment on the ReJust portal (*Registrul Electronic al Judecaiilor şi Sentinaelor*) is an electronic register of judgments created as part of the National Digital Agenda Strategy for Romania (Strategia Naionalí privind Agenda Digitalí pentru România). The portal was launched in 2019 and has become an important tool for increasing the transparency of the judicial system. The portal is a valuable tool for lawyers who can use it to find precedents, analyze judicial practice and prepare for cases. The introduction of the ReJust portal for the publication of court decisions in Romania was made possible thanks to a number of legislative changes aimed at digitalizing the judicial system. ReJust offers a wide range of features aimed at facilitating access to court decisions: (1) **search for solutions**: users can search for solutions by keywords, dates, case numbers, names of judges and other parameters; (2)

Law No. 135/2010 on the Romanian Code of Civil Procedure entered into force on February 1, 2013 and replaced the previous Code of Civil [134]Procedure of 1865, significantly modernizing the procedural rules and adapting them to modern realities. One of the key innovations of the law was the introduction of electronic means in civil proceedings.

filtering results: the portal allows you to filter search results by court type, case category and other criteria; (3) **access to the full texts of decisions** (users can familiarize themselves with the full texts of court decisions, except in cases where this is contrary to the legislation on the protection of personal data).

ReJust provides data on the number of cases reviewed, average deadlines and other indicators, which allows you to analyze the work of the judicial system. The introduction of the ReJust portal is important both for the judicial system and for society as a whole. ReJust helps increase the transparency of litigation by providing access to court decisions. This allows citizens and organizations to better understand how the judicial system works and monitor its activities. The openness of judicial decisions strengthens citizens' confidence in justice.[135]

6. Use of electronic signature. The Electronic Signature Act (Act No. 455/2001) established the legal basis for the use of electronic documents and signatures in the judicial system. The introduction of an electronic signature required the creation of a technical infrastructure that would ensure the reliable and secure transmission of documents. In Romania, the **National Electronic Signature System (SNES) was developed for this purpose,** which includes the following elements: a) **electronic platform of the court, b) integration with judicial systems, c) electronic signature.** This system provides fast and reliable transfer of documents, reducing the time and cost of their processing.

6. Search for court decisions through the Portal Jurisprudenthe. [136]According to article 151 of the Romanian CPC, parties to the proceedings may use electronic means to file documents, notifications and other procedural actions. The law also provides for the creation of a single electronic platform for interaction between courts,

---

[135]Grudtsyna L.Y. Digitalization of justice and use of electronic means in litigation in Romania//Digital law. 2025. № 1. S. 48-55.
[136]Portalul Justiției Electronice. [Electronic Resource]. URL: https://portal.just.ro.

participants in the process and other interested parties. **Portal Jurisprudenthe** provides access to the following services:

- ***Electronic filing***: Parties can file claims, motions and other documents through an online platform, significantly reducing the time and cost of delivering them.
- ***Electronic notices:*** Courts send notices of proceedings, decisions and other proceedings in electronic form, which speeds up communication between participants in the process.
- ***Online payment of court fees:*** the system allows you to pay court fees via the Internet, which simplifies financial transactions.
- Videoconferencing: courts ***may hold meetings with the participation of parties located in different geographical locations.***

In some cases, the portal system is unstable, which can lead to delays in the publication of solutions. Further improvement of the technical infrastructure is required to address this problem. Publishing solutions requires a high level of personal data protection. This requires the introduction of modern encryption and information protection technologies.

8. Electronic access to legislation through Portal Legislativ. The introduction of the Legisllativ portal in Romania was made possible by a number of legislative changes aimed at digitalizing the legal system. [137]The main regulations governing this process are: **The Law on Electronic Signature (Law No. 455/2001), the Law on Judicial Reform (2018), the Romanian Code of Civil Procedure**. The introduction of the Legislativ portal for electronic access to legislative acts in Romania has led to a number of positive results: a) **increasing the transparency of the legislative system** (publishing acts on the portal allows all interested parties to familiarize themselves with them, which increases the transparency of the legislative system), b) **increasing the availability of legal information** (process participants located in remote regions or abroad can quickly familiarize themselves with acts, which increases the availability

[137]https://www.juridice.ro/wp-content/uploads/2014/12/Strategia-Nationala-AD.pdf

of legal information), c) **reducing costs** (using the portal reduces the cost of processing paper documents and postage).

Despite the positive results, the implementation of the Legisllativ portal in Romania faced a number of challenges: (1) **digital literacy** (some participants in the process, especially older people, have difficulty using electronic systems. To solve this problem, it is necessary to conduct educational programs and provide technical support); (2) **technical failures (in** some cases, the portal system is unstable, which may lead to delays in the publication of acts. Further improvement of the technical infrastructure is required to address this problem); (3) **data confidentiality** (publication of acts requires a high level of personal data protection. This requires the introduction of modern encryption and information protection technologies). Thus, the introduction of the Legisllativ portal for electronic access to legislative acts in Romania is an important step in the digitalization of justice.

9. Conducting mediation online. The introduction of online mediation in Romania was made possible by a number of legislative changes aimed at digitalizing the legal system. The main regulations governing this process are: (1) ***the Mediation Act*** **(Act No. 192/2006).** This Act created the legal basis for the use of mediation as an alternative method of dispute resolution; (2) ***The Law on Judicial Reform*** **(2018).** This law provided for the introduction of online mediation as part of a comprehensive reform aimed at modernizing the judicial system; (3) ***Romanian Code of Civil Procedure***. In 2020, the code was amended to allow online mediation. These regulations have created a legal framework for the use of online mediation, ensuring its legal force and recognition in judicial practice.

The introduction of online mediation required the creation of a technical infrastructure that would ensure reliable and secure data transfer. In Romania, the ***National Online Mediation System (SNOM) has been developed for this purpose,*** which includes the following elements: (1) **an electronic platform.** each mediator has access to a centralized platform through which mediation can be carried out; (2)

integration with judicial systems. The platform is integrated with the main judicial systems, which allows automatic loading of dispute data; (3) **electronic signature.** Agreements reached as a result of mediation are signed by the electronic signature of the parties, which ensures their authenticity. This system provides fast and reliable data transfer, reducing the time and cost of their processing.[138]

The introduction of online mediation in Romania has led to a number of positive results: firstly, it is ***an increase in the availability of mediation.The*** online platform allows parties located in remote regions or abroad to participate in mediation, which increases the availability of this method of dispute resolution; ***secondly, reducing the time for resolving disputes.*** Online mediation allows you to speed up the process of resolving disputes, which helps to reduce the time for consideration of cases in courts; thirdly, ***cost reduction***. The use of the online platform reduces the cost of organizing and conducting mediation, including transport and administrative costs.

However, the introduction of online mediation has also faced a number of challenges, including low levels of digital literacy among some participants in the process and technical failures in the system. The introduction of online mediation in Romania is an important step in the digitalization of justice. This innovation helps to increase the availability of alternative dispute resolution methods, the effectiveness of the judicial system and reduce costs. However, to fully realize the potential of online mediation, it is necessary to solve a number of problems related to digital literacy, technical infrastructure and data protection. The experience of Romania may be useful for other countries that plan to implement similar systems in their judicial systems.

10. Using artificial intelligence (AI) to analyze court decisions. The introduction of AI technologies into the Romanian judicial system was made possible by a number of legislative changes aimed at digitalizing justice. The main regulations governing this process are: (1) ***the Electronic Signature Act (Act No. 455/2001).*** This

---

[138]Grudtsyna L.Y. Digitalization of justice and use of electronic means in litigation in Romania//Digital law. 2025. № 1. S. 48-55.

Act created the legal basis for the use of electronic documents and signatures in the judicial system; (2) ***The Law on Judicial Reform (2018).*** This law provided for the introduction of AI technologies as part of a comprehensive reform aimed at modernizing the judicial system; (3) ***Romanian Code of Civil Procedure*** In 2020, the Code was amended to allow the use of AI for the analysis of court decisions. These regulations created a legal framework for the use of AI, ensuring its legal force and recognition in judicial practice.

The introduction of AI technologies required the creation of a technical infrastructure that would provide reliable and secure analysis of court decisions. In Romania, the **National Judicial Decision Analysis System (SNASD)** was developed for this, which uses machine learning and natural language processing (NLP) algorithms to analyze the texts of judicial decisions, identify key legal principles and trends. [139]This system provides fast and reliable data processing, reducing the time and cost of their analysis.[140]

The article reviews the processes of introducing electronic services into the judicial system of Romania, including the process of electronic filing of claims in Romania as a key element of the digitalization of justice. Statistical data, the dynamics of the introduction of electronic services, their impact on the effectiveness of the judicial system and the availability of justice for citizens are analyzed. Graphs illustrating the growth in the use of electronic means for filing claims are [141]given, as well as the challenges and prospects for further development are discussed.

It was concluded that the use of videoconferencing in court hearings was an important step in the digitalization of justice in Romania. Statistics show a steady increase in the use of this technology, [142]which contributes to the efficiency and accessibility of the judicial system. The introduction of the Jurisprudenthe portal for

---

[139]Strategia Națională privind Agenda Digitală pentru România (2014).
[140]Stanciu, R. (2019). The Impact of Electronic Means in Civil Proceedings: The Romanian Experience. Romanian Journal of Comparative Law, 10(3), 78-92.
[141]Portalul Justiției Electronice. [Electronic Resource]. URL: https://portal.just.ro.
[142]Portalul Justiției Electronice. [Electronic Resource]. URL: https://portal.just.ro.

judicial solutions in Romania is an important step in the digitalization of justice. This innovation contributes to improving the transparency of the judicial system, the availability of justice and reducing costs. However, to fully realize the potential of the portal, it is necessary to solve a number of problems related to digital literacy, technical infrastructure and the protection of personal data.

The introduction of an electronic filing system in Romania has led to a number of positive results: first, improving the availability of justice (electronic filing of claims allows plaintiffs in remote regions or abroad to quickly file claims, which increases the availability of justice), secondly, reducing the time for consideration of cases (electronic filing of claims allows to speed up the process of filing and registering claims, which helps to reduce the time for consideration of cases), thirdly, reducing the administrative burden (the use of an electronic system reduces the cost of processing paper documents and postage, which reduces the administrative burden on the judicial system).

However, the introduction of electronic filing has also faced a number of challenges, including low levels of digital literacy among some stakeholders and technical failures in the system. A number of challenges related to digital literacy, technical infrastructure and data protection need to be addressed in order to fully realize the potential of electronic notifications. The experience of Romania may be useful for other countries that plan to implement similar systems in their judicial systems.

The introduction of AI technologies for analyzing court decisions in Romania has led to a number of positive results: (1) ***improving*** the efficiency of the judicial system.AI allows you to automatically analyze large volumes of court decisions, which helps to shorten the time for consideration of cases and improve the quality of law enforcement; (2) ***improving access to legal information.The*** platform provides lawyers, judges and citizens with access to analytical data, which increases the transparency of the judicial system; (3) ***ensuring uniformity of judicial practice.*** AI helps to identify contradictions in court decisions and contributes to the formation of a single judicial practice. However, AI adoption has also faced a number of challenges, including low levels of digital literacy among some participants in the process and technical failures in the system.[143]

In **Slovenia**, one of the leaders in the digitalization of justice in Europe, the central, highly developed and integrated platform of Slovenian e-justice is the Single Platform e-Sodstvo (e-Justice). The e-Sodstvo platform covers almost all aspects of Slovenian legal proceedings. This is a key digital justice infrastructure recognized as one of the most advanced in the EU. It provides end-to-end digitalization of court processes, uniting all participants in the system (courts, lawyers, prosecutors, citizens, business) through a single portal - a centralized entrance for all services (filing documents, access to cases, registers, payment of duties). Access for citizens, lawyers, state bodies is carried out through electronic identification (e-ID, digital certificates).

Slovenia has a well-developed electronic document management system. All claims, complaints, petitions are filed online, lawyers are obliged to use this system. Automatic distribution of court calls, decisions and definitions to the participants of the process. All documents are certified by a qualified electronic signature (built into the system). All case materials (protocols, evidence, decisions) are stored in digital format (electronic case (e-Akt). Judges and participants in the process have round-the-clock access to the current version of the case, which eliminates duplication of paper carriers. Integration with state registers and databases was carried out - the platform is connected with such state databases as:

- AJPES (Central Register of Companies): data on legal entities.
- Land cadastre: real estate information.
- Mortgage register: mortgage encumbrances.
- Population register: verification of personal data.
- Automation of judicial procedures.

[143]Popescu, A. (2021). Digital Transformation of the Judiciary in Romania: Challenges and Opportunities. Journal of Legal Studies, 15(2), 45-60.

The system automatically assigns a judge, excluding manual intervention (random allocation of cases). Integration with video conferencing systems (VCC), notifications of the timing of procedural actions were carried out, all court decisions are published anonymously in the public domain, which ensures the openness and transparency of legal proceedings.

Table 3. Advantages of e-Sodstvo in Slovenia.

Aspect	Effect
Process Speed	Reduction of case processing time by 30-50% (less "paper" delays).
Resource Savings	Refusal of paper, mail, physical storage of archives.
Availability	24-hour access to cases from anywhere in the country.
Transparency	Reducing corruption risks by automating key solutions.
Environmental friendliness	Reducing the court system's carbon footprint.

Along with the positive effects of the implementation of the e-Sodstvo system in Slovenia, there are certain, still unresolved problems. Among them:

A. Cybersecurity (risks of hacker attacks (requires continuous investment in protection).

B. Digital divide (not all citizens (especially the elderly) are ready for online interaction).

B. Technical support (legacy maintenance and staff training required).

D. Legal barriers (adaptation of procedural codes to the digital environment).

Thus, e-Sodstvo is not just an "electronic archive," but an ecosystem of end-to-end digital justice, which has become a benchmark for the EU. Its success is based on: a single architecture (without "patchwork" automation), mandatory use for professionals, deep integration with state registers. Slovenia has proved that a full transition to e-justice is possible even in a small country.[144]

Table 4. How e-Akt works: stages of business.

Stage	Actions in e-Sodstvo
1. Filing a claim	• The plaintiff/lawyer uploads the claim + evidence through the portal.
2. Registration	• The system automatically assigns a case number, creates e-Akt.
3. Appointment of a judge	• The algorithm randomly distributes the case (eliminates manual influence).
4. Notice to Parties	• Automatic dispatch of electronic summons with access to e-Akt.
5. Document Exchange	• All motions, objections, additional proofs are uploaded to e-Akt.
6. Meeting	• The judge studies the materials online. HQS is integrated into the system.
7. Decision	• The judge signs the CEP verdict → is automatically published in e-Akt.
8. Appeal	• The complaint is submitted through e-Sodstvo → the case is referred to a higher court without duplication.
9. Archiving	• e-Akt is stored in a secure cloud for 30 + years. Paper copies are not created.

Protection against abuse in e-Akt: version control system (records all changes, who/when edited the document), CEP for each action (loading the document, signing the decision, etc.), as well as backup (data is stored in three geographically distributed data centers). In practice, the following problems with using e-Akt are possible:

[144]Grudtsyna L.Y. Digitalization of justice in Romania and Slovenia: theoretical and legal review//Humanities. High School. 2025. № 1. S. 28-35.

A. Technical failures: Rare but critical (e.g. system unavailability in a DDoS attack in 2021).

B. Digital illiteracy: Older lawyers or citizens experience difficulties (solution: free courses at courts).

B. Limitations for criminal cases: Complex cases with physical evidence are partly conducted in a hybrid format.

Thus, Slovenian e-Akt is not just a "scan of the case," but a digital judicial environment, where each stage is regulated by law. This is an example of the successful transformation of traditional justice through: a rigid legislative framework (mandatory ES, priority of e-documents); deep integration of all participants in e-Sodstvo; technological reliability (encryption, audit, redundancy).

Achievements:

1. High degree of digitalization: Slovenia is recognized as one of the most advanced EU countries in the field of e-justice. The system covers most courts and types of cases.

2. Efficiency and speed: Significant reduction of time for administrative procedures, transfer of documents, search for information. Acceleration of proceedings.

3. Transparency and accessibility: Easy access to information on the progress of cases (for participants), court decisions, registries. Convenient tools for citizens and business.

4. Cost reduction: Savings on paper, postage, physical storage of cases.

5. Convenience for professionals: An integrated system greatly simplifies the work of lawyers and prosecutors.

The outstanding issues to date are:

Legacy integration: The need to maintain and integrate legacy systems with the new platform.

Continuous development and funding: Continuous investment is required in upgrading, security and adding new features.

Cybersecurity: The constant threat of cyberattacks requires serious measures to protect critical infrastructure.

Digital inclusion: Making the system accessible to all citizens, including the elderly and those without digital skills or access to the internet (although the infrastructure in Slovenia is well developed).

Legal aspects: Adaptation of procedural legislation to a fully electronic process.

Table 5. Comparison of aspects of digitalization of legal proceedings in Romania and Slovenia.

№	Characteristic	Romania	Slovenia
1.	Maturity Level	Medium, developing, uneven	High, one of the leaders of the EU
2.	Key Platform	Portalul Just.ro, disparate systems (e-proces, e-dosar)	Single integrated e-Sodstvo platform
3.	Electronic Filing	Partly, in pilot courts/for lawyers	Everywhere, mostly mandatory for lawyers
4.	Electronic Case	Implemented (e-dosar)	Fully implemented (e-Akt)
5.	Access to information	Limited/Incomplete via Portal	Wide and convenient via e-Sodstvo
6.	Transparency (status of cases)	Limited	High (for process participants)
7.	Use of video conferencing	Wide	Wide
8.	Electronic registries	Develop, access partial	Well developed, available online (AJPES, etc.)

Note that Slovenia demonstrates an example of successful and integrated digitalization of justice. The single e-Sodstvo platform has become the basis for efficient, transparent and convenient electronic proceedings covering most proceedings. This is the result of consistent policy and investment. Romania is at an earlier stage. Although Romanian legislation is constantly improving (Just.ro, e-proces), the implementation process faces serious difficulties: heterogeneity of implementation, technical limitations, resistance to change and insufficient integration of systems. There is movement forward, but Romania is still far from the maturity level of the Slovenian system. Both countries continue to develop digital justice, understanding its key importance for the modern state and citizens' trust in the judicial system. Slovenia's experience is an important reference point for Romania and other countries in the region.

REFERENCES

Russian-speaking sources

1. For more information on the French New Code of Civil Procedure and the French Code of Civil Procedure of 1806, see Dictionary of Basic Terms in the following publication: French Commercial Code. (Preface, translation, supplement, reference apparatus and comments by V. N. Zakhvataev). - Volters Kluver, M. 2008. - S. 755-756; 856 — 857.

2. Law No. 135/2010 on the Romanian Code of Civil Procedure entered into force on February 1, 2013 and replaced the previous Code of Civil Procedure of 1865, significantly modernizing the procedural rules and adapting them to modern realities. One of the key innovations of the law was the introduction of electronic means in civil proceedings.

3. PRC. Laws. Civil Procedure Code: Law of the People's Republic of China: [adopted on April 9, 1991: as amended on November 28, 2007]. — URL: https://chinalawinfo. ru/procedural_law/law_civil_procedure (date of circulation: 04. 05. 2025).

4. Kalashnikova S.I. Mediation in the field of civil jurisdiction/S.I. Kalashnikov - M.: InfotropicMedia, 2011. — 304 c.

5. Ablaeva E. B. "Rule of law" in the work of international organizations//Gaps in Russian legislation. 2017. №7. P. 199.

6. Bryantseva O. V., Soldatkina O. L. Comparative analysis of foreign electronic justice systems//Vestnik PAGS. 2019. №6. S. 36-47.

7. Garipov T.I., Morugina N.A. Analysis of foreign experience in the use of electronic criminal case in the procedural activities of the preliminary investigation and court bodies//Bulletin of the Kazan Law Institute of the Ministry of Internal Affairs of Russia. 2021. №4 (46) . S. 585-594.

8. Goshin V. A. Judicial precedent as a source of European Union law//Gaps in Russian legislation. 2015. №4. S. 294.

9. Grudtsyna L. Yu. Issues of the organization of electronic justice in the European Union//Research Institute for Education and Law. 2025. № 1 - 3. S. 14-18.
10.Grudtsyna L. Yu. Predictive proceedings: a comparative analysis of the law enforcement practice of the USA, Germany, France and China//International Scientific Bulletin. 2025. № 4. S. 162-167.
11.Grudtsyna L. Yu. Judicial precedent and judicial law-making: public - legal aspect//Education and law. 2024. № 8. S. 98-103.
12.Grudtsyna L. Yu. Digitalization of justice in the European Union//International Scientific Bulletin. 2025. № 7. S. 198-204.
13.Grudtsyna L. Yu. Digitalization of justice in the kingdom of Spain//Humanities. High School. 2025. № 2. S. 35-40.
14.Grudtsyna L. Yu. Digitalization of justice in Latvia and Lithuania: theoretical - legal review//Humanities. High School. 2025. № 1. S. 59-64.
15.Grudtsyna L. Yu. Digitalization of justice in Romania and Slovenia: theoretical - legal review//Humanities. High School. 2025. № 1. S. 28-35.
16.Grudtsyna L. Yu. Digitalization of justice and the use of electronic means in litigation in Romania//Digital law. 2025. № 1. S. 48-55.
17.Grudtsyna L. Yu. Digitalization of legal proceedings on the example of some countries of the European Union//Academic Science. 2025. № 1. S. 65-72.
18.Grudtsyna L. Yu. Digital Justice in Spain//Digital Law. 2024. № 4. S. 46-48.
19.Grudtsyna L. Yu. Digital Justice in Estonia//Digital Law. 2024. № 4. S. 59-65.
20.Grudtsyna L. Yu. Electronic Justice in China//International Scientific Bulletin. 2025. № 2. P. 28.
21.Grudtsyna L. Yu. Electronic Justice in the USA//Economics and Law. XXI century. 2025. № 1. S. 35-38.
22.Grudtsyna L. Yu. Electronic justice in the USA: the legal framework for transformation in the context of digitalization//Digital law. 2025. № 1. S. 11-15.
23.Danshin A.V. Institute of Mediation in Traditional China (X-XIX centuries) ./A.V. Danshin//Historical, philosophical, political and legal sciences, cultural

studies and art history. Questions of theory and practice. — 2014. — 12 (50) . — c. 42 - 46.

24.Dragilev E.V., Dragileva L.L., Drovaleva L.S., Palamarchuk S.A. Informatization of the judicial system of China//Legal science. 2022. № 8. S. 54-59.

25.Konopiy A. S. Digital Transformation of the State and Law of China//North Caucasian Legal Bulletin. 2021. № 3. S. 72-77.

26.Korosteleva Yu. A., Simonovsky D. A. Legal regulation of mediation in China: a brief review//International Research Journal. 2023. № 6 (132) . P. 12.

27.Kurlyshev A.O. Digitalization and artificial intelligence in criminal proceedings: problems and challenges//Public service and personnel. 2024. № 1. S. 295-298.

28.Lipatova T. B. Implementation of the principles of civil procedural law in the framework of electronic justice//Bulletin of the SSLA. 2022. №4 (147) . S. 100-107.

29.Malko A.V., Elistratova V.V. Problems of the formation of the judicial system of the Eurasian Economic Union//Socio-political sciences. 2017. №3. S. 43-47.

30.Ovsyannikova T. A., Firsova I. A. The main elements of the juvenile justice system in China//MNIZH. 2021. № 10 - 2 (112) . S. 176-178.

31.Sidelnik I. M. Foreign experience in using procedural presumptions//Theory and practice of social development. 2018. №7. S. 118-121.

32.Sobenin A. A. Integrated Criminal Justice Information Systems//Bulletin of O. E. Kutafin University. 2020. №10 (74) . S. 158-166.

33.Sutormina L. A. Readmission as an instrument of the immigration policy of the European Union (on the example of a readmission agreement with Russia)//Bulletin of Moscow University. Series 25. International relations and world politics. 2011. №1. S. 149-162.

34.Tagirov Z. I. Modern activities of the police of the European Union to counter terrorism//Bulletin of the Kazan Law Institute of the Ministry of Internal Affairs of Russia. 2019. №4 (38) . S. 426-430.

35.Khoroshko I.V. Foreign experience of electronic form of civil proceedings on the example of the Republic of Singapore and the People's Republic of China: history of origin and current state//Person: crime and punishment. 2022. № 2. S. 183-187.

36.Official website: https ://e. teismas. lt. URL: https://e. (date of access: 05.10.2025).

37.The GDPR replaced the 95/46/EC Directive and established uniform strict rules for the processing of personal data within the European Union.

38.In China, more than 80% of disputes that arise do not reach the court (filing a lawsuit and litigation) and are resolved by alternative methods (including extrajudicial mediation). См. , например: Yuwen Li, The Judicial System and Reform in Post - Mao China: Stumbling Towards Justice (The Rule of Law in China and Comparative Perspectives) Routledge Press, 2014, Chapter 5, p. 239.

39.Report on the implementation of the plan (2023): Ministry of Justice Spain.

40.European Commission. Report on the digitalization of justice in EU countries (2022).

41.Report of the Romanian Ministry of Justice on the implementation of the electronic notification (2021).

42.Report of the Romanian Ministry of Justice on the implementation of electronic filing of claims (2021).

Foreign sources

43.Bianchi, F. (2023) . "Data Protection in Digital Courts: A European Perspective". European Law Journal.

44.Brown, T. (2023) . "The Digital Divide in Access to Justice: Lessons from China". Yale Journal of International Law.

45.Chen, J. (2022) . "Digital Transformation of Justice in China: Challenges and Opportunities". Journal of Legal Technology. China Law Review.

46.Johnson, R. (2021) . "Internet Courts and the Future of Justice: A Global Perspective". Harvard Journal of Law & Technology.

47.Müller, S. (2021) . "Digital Justice: Lessons from China's Internet Courts". European Journal of Legal Studies.

48.Popescu, A. (2021) . Digital Transformation of the Judiciary in Romania: Challenges and Opportunities. Journal of Legal Studies, 15 (2) , 45 - 60.

49.Smith, E. (2022) . "Ethical Implications of AI in Judicial Decision - Making". Stanford Law Review.

50.Stanciu, R. (2019) . The Impact of Electronic Means in Civil Proceedings: The Romanian Experience. Romanian Journal of Comparative Law, 10 (3) , 78 - 92.

51.Wang, Y. (2020) . "Blockchain Technology in Judicial Systems: Case Study of China". International Journal of Law and Information Technology.

52.Zhang, H. (2023) . "Smart Courts and the Future of Justice in China". Asian Journal of Legal Studies.

53.Grudtsyna L. Yu. Digitalization of justice in the USA: case management electronic case files (CMECF) and public access to court electronic records (PACER)//Law and management. 2025. № 2. S. 112-117.

54.Changes in Online Access to Oregon Circuit Court Information due to June 8, 2015 Oregon eCourt implementation events / https://www. osbar. org/_docs/eCourt/OCM_Accesstocourt. pdf. URL: https://www. (date of access: 05.10.2025).

55.https://azcourthelp. org/azturbocourt. URL: https://azcourthelp. (date of access: 05.10.2025).

56.https://capessokol. com/insights/out - with - the - oldin - with - the - new - missouri - efiling - system/. URL: https://capessokol. (date of access: 05.10.2025).

57.https://e - courts. org/agenda/. URL: https ://e (date of access: 05.10.2025).

58.https://efile. illinoiscourts. gov. URL: https://efile. (date of access: 05.10.2025).

59.https://efileus. com/eFileLA/. URL: https://efileus. (date of access: 05.10.2025).

60.https://levyclerk. com/wp - content/uploads/Florida - ePortal - and - eFiling - FAQs. pdf. URL: https://levyclerk. (date of access: 05.10.2025).

61.https://sf. courts. ca. gov/online - services/e - filing. URL: https://sf. (date of access: 05.10.2025).
62.https://themagzine. co. uk/2024/09/03/oregon - ecourts - modernization/. URL: https://themagzine. (date of access: 05.10.2025).
63.https://vermontrepublic. org/new - court - e - filing - system - in - vermont/. URL: https://vermontrepublic. (date of access: 05.10.2025).
64.https://www. cacd. uscourts. gov/e - filing. URL: https://www. (date of access: 05.10.2025).
65.https://www. gabar. org/efiling. cfm. URL: https://www. (date of access: 05.10.2025).
66.https://www. juridice. ro/wp - content/uploads/2014/12/Strategia - Nationala - AD. pdf. URL: https://www. (date of access: 05.10.2025).
67.https://www. onelegal. com/blog/navigating - the - new - era - of - efiling - in - nevada - with - one - legal/. URL: https://www. (date of access: 05.10.2025).
68.https://www. paralegalbrief. com/efiling/nebraska/. URL: https://www. (date of access: 05.10.2025).
69.https://www. revenue. state. mn. us/free - electronic - filing. URL: https://www. (date of access: 05.10.2025).
70.https://www.ritvus.com/news/ehlektronnoe_pravosudie_v_ssha_zarubezhnyj_opyt/2018 - 07 - 25 - 171. URL: https://www. (date of access: 05.10.2025).
71.https://www.utcourts.gov/en/legal-help/legal-help/procedures/filing/efiling /district.html. URL: https://www. (date of access: 05.10.2025).
72.https://www. vermontjudiciary. org/about - vermont - judiciary/electronic - access/electronic - filing. URL: https://www. (date of access: 05.10.2025).
73.https://www. whitehouse. gov/presidential - actions/2025/01/establishing - and - implementing - the - presidents - department - of - government - efficiency/. URL: https://www. (date of access: 05.10.2025).
74.Pennsylvania Rules of Appellate Procedure (Public Access Policy of the Unified Judicial System of Pennsylvania: Case Records of the Appellate and Trial Courts; No. 126 Misc. Doc. No. 3 [47 Pa. B. 7851] [Saturday, December 30, 2017]) /

https://www.lawcatalog.com/media/productattach/p/a/pa_state_court_rules_ch01_ rules_of_appellate_procedure.pdf. URL: https://www. (date of access: 05.10.2025).

75.Portalul Justiției Electronice. [Electronic Resource]. URL: https://portal. just. ro (date of access: 05.10.2025).

76.Ten Courts of Appeals Move to CM/ECF / http://www. uscourts. gov/News/TheThirdBranch/06-05-01/Ten_Courts_of_Appeals_Move_t o_CM_ECF. aspx. URL: http://www. (date of access: 05.10.2025).

77.How the courts of the world refuse paper. URL: https://ejustice. cnews. en/articles/2016 - 05 - 13 kaksudymiraotkazyvayutsyaotbumagi (date of access: 05.10.2025).

78.Official address: https ://www. latvija. lv. URL: https://www. (date of access: 05.10.2025).

79.Official CGPJ website: https ://www. poderjudicial. es. URL: https://www. (date of access: 05.10.2025).

80.Official website: https ://manas. tiesas. lv. URL: https://manas. (date of access: 05.10.2025).

81.BVerfG, Urteil vom 15. 12. 2019 — 1 BvR 2765/16.

82.CNIL, "L'IA dans la justice" (2021).

83.E - Estonia. (2023) . Digital Court System.

84.e - Estonia. How Estonia's X - Road Powers Digital Government. 2022.

85.eIDAS Regulation (EU) No 910/2014.

86.Estonian Information System Authority. X - Road Technical Specifications. 2020.

87.Estonian Judiciary Annual Report 2023.

88.European Commission. "Digitalisation of Justice" (2022).

89.European Commission. (2020) . Digitalisation of justice in the EU.

90.European Commission. e - Justice Report. 2021.

91.Krull L. Secure Data Exchange in E - Government. Springer, 2018.

92.Legea nr. 135/2010 privind Codul de procedură civilă.

93.Ley 18/2011, de 5 de julio, reguladora del uso de las tecnologías de la información y la comunicación en la Administración de Justicia.
94.Li, X. (2021) . "Artificial Intelligence in Chinese Courts: A New Era of Justice".
95.OECD. Digital Government in Estonia. 2019.
96.On January 20, 2025 Donald Trump issued an executive order reorganizing and renaming USDS as the United States DOGE Service, where DOGE stands for Department of Government Efficiency. Trump subsequently appointed billionaire and SpaceX owner Elon Musk to manage the new department. The executive order also established a temporary organization within the United States DOGE Service, called the U. S. DOGE Service Temporary Organization (USDSTO).
97.Plan de Transformación Digital de la Justicia 2019 — 2023. CGPJ.
98.Strategia Națională privind Agenda Digitală pentru România (2014).
99.Tamm M. "e - Justice in Estonia". Springer, 2021.
100. The AZTurboCourt website includes links to the Arizona Judicial Branch's online services, known as eServices. One of the featured online services is electronic filing, commonly referred to as eFiling. The AZTurboCourt. gov eFiling service guides filers through the process of preparing case submissions by asking a series of questions in an interview - like fashion.
101. The ePortal is a web site that provides eFiling and eRecording capability to users with a single statewide login. Users may utilize the ePortal web interface to submit documents to Clerks and Recorders. The ePortal also supports automated interfaces with other submitter systems. The ePortal supports transmissions to/from the local case/recording systems using national XML standards. The ePortal also provides electronic notifications and service on behalf of filers.
102. Yuwen Li, The Judicial System and Reform in Post - Mao China: Stumbling Towards Justice (The Rule of Law in China and Comparative Perspectives) Routledge Press, 2014, Chapter 5, p. 239.

www.ingramcontent.com/pod-product-compliance
Lightning Source LLC
LaVergne TN
LVHW022112200926
848481LV00003B/1156
* 9 7 9 8 8 9 9 6 6 3 5 3 6 *